BUILDINGS OF
IRISH
TOWNS

for Conor, Clíodhna and Gráinne

SPONSORS

The Arts Council/An Chomhairle Ealaíon
Ove Arup and Partners
Bailieborough Co-Operative Society Ltd.
Barry Associates
Bowman and Quaid
Burke Kennedy Doyle and Partners
Costello Murray and Beaumont
Delaney McVeigh and Pike
The Irish Planning Institute
Arthur Lardner and Partners
Peter Legge and Partners
Fergal and Brid McCabe
James O'Beirne
Anthony and Barbara O'Neill
John Paul and Co. (Dublin)
Pembroke Estates
Robinson Keefe and Devane
Philip N. Shaffrey and Partners
Tegral Limited
P. J. Walls (Dublin) Ltd.

Previous page 1 Newry, Co. Down, The Mall –
canal warehouse, built in brick, with an unusually elegant facade
reflecting the good taste and design skill of the builder.

The cover illustration shows, left to right, starting on back cover;
Front Row: houses, Eden Road, Birr, Co. Offaly; Orange Hall,
Hamilton Road, Bangor, Co. Down; house, John's Gate Street, Wexford;
shop and house, Main Street, Carrick-on-Shannon, Co. Leitrim;
The Stag's Head, Dame Court, Dublin.
Middle Row: railway station, Thurles, Co. Tipperary; Court-house,
the Square, Bantry, Co. Cork.
Back Row: Church of Ireland church, The Diamond,
Ballycastle, Co. Antrim; town hall, Fair Street, Drogheda, Co. Louth.
Catholic church, Callan, Co. Kilkenny;
jail, Cormack Street, Tullamore, Co. Offaly.

BUILDINGS OF
IRISH TOWNS

Treasures of Everyday Architecture

Patrick & Maura Shaffrey

The Architectural Press

LONDON

First published in Ireland by The O'Brien Press Ltd.
20 Victoria Road, Dublin 6, 1983.
First published in Britain by The Architectural Press Ltd.
9 Queen Anne's Gate, London SW1H 9BY, 1984.
First published in the United States of America by Templegate Publishers
302 East Adams, P.O. Box 5152, Springfield, Illinois 62705, 1984.

© Patrick and Maura Shaffrey

British Library Cataloguing in Publication Data
Shaffrey, Patrick
Buildings of Irish towns
1. Cities and towns - Ireland
I. Title II. Shaffrey, Maura
721'.09173'2 NA2750

ISBN 0-86278-045-4 The O'Brien Press
ISBN 0-85139-759-X The Architectural Press
ISBN 0-87243-126-6 Templegate Press

Text by Patrick Shaffrey.
Illustrations by Maura Shaffrey. Photographs by Patrick Shaffrey unless otherwise stated.
Book design by Michael O'Brien assisted by Íde Ní Laoghaire.
Edited by Íde Ní Laoghaire assisted by Fiona McKinney. Copy-edited by Siobhán Parkinson.
Typesetting by Leaders, Swords, Co. Dublin.
Printed by Irish Printers Ltd., Dublin.

ILLUSTRATIONS

The authors and publisher wish to thank the following for permission to reproduce maps, photographs or to make
drawings from original materials. All remaining photographs and drawings are by the authors.
CIE 2, 146; National Library of Ireland 4, 51, 122, 139; Office of Public Works 6, 104;
Trinity College Dublin 11; St Joseph's Cambridge 18; Pembroke Estates Dublin 19, 25;
Ordnance Survey Office, Dublin 21, 64, 106, 110; Bord Failte 23; Kilkenny Corporation and C. Ó Cochlain, Kilkenny 27;
Drogheda Museum 34; Ulster Folk Museum 42; Northern Ireland Housing Executive 52;
Ballinasloe UDC 58; IPA Dublin 72; Ordnance Survey Office, Belfast 73;
Parish Priest, Callan 77; B. Rhatigan, Sligo 75, 79; Cork Corporation 80;
Dublin Corporation 81; Cavan Co. Council 86; Cork Co. Council 88;
North Tipperary Co. Council 90; Sligo Corporation 92; Naas UDC 95;
Dublin Co. Council 96; Waterford Co. Library 102; An Cosantóir 107;
Dept. of Defence 109; Lyons, Sligo 117; Cash's, Cork 125;
Bank of Ireland 128, 129; McKenzies, Cork 134; Limerick Savings Bank 137;
Minch Norton, Muine Bheag 144; Commissioner of Lights 155.

Contents

Preface

Buildings are an expression of civilisation and values. From the primitive structures of the first settlers, the great chambers at Newgrange, the medieval cathedrals and abbeys and the eighteenth-century streets and squares to the new house which will be occupied next week, buildings provide the settings for great public occasions and for private and intimate events which take place in one's own home. There are many types of buildings. The great buildings, through their artistic splendours or structural inventiveness, have made significant contributions to the progress of civilisation and add to the dignity and prestige of community and national well-being. They have also influenced the great mass of ordinary buildings which each generation erects for its own needs. When the great buildings are, unfortunately, mutilitated or destroyed, there is – and quite rightly so – heated debate and public concern, though too often not as widespread as one would welcome, – but the 'little ones' can be removed or changed without a murmur.

We have been fortunate that our work as architects and town planners has allowed us to travel throughout Ireland, and thus we have become aware of the great heritage of buildings which this generation possesses. Many times we have been literally 'stopped in our tracks' by the sheer beauty and architectural qualities of ordinary buildings: sometimes by a country cottage, whose proportions, aesthetic quality, and simplicity of presentation suggest a 'master's hand'; or perhaps by a traditional shop, standing out with dignity and splendour in contrast to crudely modernised neighbours; or it might be the parish church, where the great architectural styles were modified but not debased by local interpretations. Unfortunately, we were too often appalled by the numerous examples of insensitive attempts to improve, modify or extend many ordinary buildings which possess great charm and architectural dignity. Such clumsiness was usually caused by a lack of knowledge and awareness. Sometimes the owners were pleased with their handiwork; occasionally they blamed their advisers for failure. They often accepted however, that there were architecturally more acceptable ways – and not necessarily more expensive ways – of improving their building.

We were disappointed by the general lack of knowledge about such matters as the architectural style, quality of craftsmanship, date of erection, or the names of the architect and builder of many buildings. The buildings of a neighbourhood were taken for granted, when, in many cases, they are often among its glories.

We hope, through this book, to share our knowledge, as far as it goes, our concern for and our appreciation of these buildings. The book is written primarily for lay people and so we have avoided, wherever possible, detailed technical descriptions or rarefied architectural terms. We hope, in particular, that the illustrations have captured the vitality and quality of the buildings which we have come to know and love. For every building illustrated we could have chosen dozens more, equally interesting and equally of architectural significance. We hope that readers will more readily recognise the buildings of quality in their own town or district and be able to appreciate their architectural, historical, and social significance in a more rewarding way. If we succeed in this, our goal will have been achieved.

Many people and organisations contributed to the publication of this work. We would particularly like to thank our sponsors who supported our work so enthusiastically. We thank the Heritage Trust for a grant towards research work; Bord Fáilte Eireann, and especially George Bagnall on whose behalf we had many opportunities of travelling throughout Ireland; those people who while working with us and sharing the day-to-day problems of private practice helped out on this project, which often for long periods threatened to take over our organisation – Valerie Bond, Gráinne Shaffrey, Cyril O'Neill, Derry O'Connell and especially our colleagues Kathleen Murphy, who was the secretarial powerhouse behind the project, and Aidan Nolan who contributed to the preparation of the black and white drawings, specifically nos. 72, 92, 101, 109, 127, 117, 144.

We thank the many people and organisations both North and South who gladly helped with information – indeed one of the joys in writing a book of this sort is the contact you make with people from all parts of Ireland and from all walks of life; the O'Brien Press, and especially Michael and Valerie O'Brien, Íde Ní Laoghaire, Fiona McKinney and Tina Kelly; Gordon and Evan Smith for photographic advice and assistance; Declan Grehan for encouragement at a crucial state; Ken Mawhinney whose comments on the draft text were extremely helpful; Philip N. Shaffrey and Partners for secretarial help; Billy Houlihan, Colin Hatrick, Daphne Henshaw and Hugh Dixon and Lewis Clohessy who helped in various ways.

Above all, we would like to thank those owners and custodians of buildings who allowed us to photograph and measure and sent us specific information but whose buildings unfortunately through sheer weight of numbers it was not possible to illustrate. We hope that they will recognise that their buildings are also a vital part of our heritage and are included in spirit if not in fact.

Chapter One

Local Architecture

Architecture is traditionally one of the features that distinguish societies and cultures from each other. This distinctiveness is seen not only in the important monuments and buildings or in the grand streets and squares of great cities, but also, indeed more especially, in local buildings such as farm houses, cottages and churches in the countryside, and small shops, houses and workshops in towns and villages. Such buildings reflect the tastes and attitudes of society. They are influenced by local economic conditions, social and cultural attitudes and site topography. They are also influenced by major developments in architectural style. Even the smallest town house may have its front doorway in the grand manner, using architectural details from the classical period or motifs in a more romantic idiom: the great architectural theories and fashions are modified by local interpretation.

One result of modern social and technological change is that societies and cultures are becoming similar. However, centralisation of activities and growing conformity of social and cultural habits have now created their own reaction and the search for distinctiveness is increasing all the time. There has also been a reaction against modern architecture, particularly against the large-scale developments that are shaping the form of cities and towns, and in the process making everything look the same. There is now a growing appreciation of older architectural styles and building techniques, and particularly of how they were affected by local design and craftsmanship and how they reflected a distinctive way of life. In the quest for the retention of national and indeed regional cultures the quality of local archi-tecture is of vital importance. There is always the danger that a search for identity can lead to petty nationalism, but if approached in an open and positive way the identification of different traditions creates a mutual respect between cultures: the Irish farmhouse is different from its French counterpart but is in no way inferior, or indeed superior, for all that.

Architecture is an important aspect of the culture of any region or country in the same way as its language, music, art and literature. In Ireland the significance of architecture was ignored for many generations. The greatest phase of architecture and town building occurred in the eighteenth and early nineteenth centuries. In the Republic particularly this period is associated with foreign rule. It is only comparatively recently that the qualities, distinctiveness, indeed greatness, of the architecture created in those years have been appreciated. The impressive Georgian buildings in Dublin and other cities and the fine country houses and estates were mostly designed, built, and lived in by Irish people, who were, generally speaking, proud of their Irishness, irrespective of their religious or political viewpoints.

If there was uncertainty about the great buildings, the general mass of buildings was more or less ignored. But it is often these buildings that give character and distinctiveness to towns, cities and the countryside. Many towns and villages may not have a single building of architectural or historic importance, yet they are exceptionally pleasant places. The ordinary buildings, which were built by and are still used by ordinary people, display local differences and distinctiveness in design and craftsmanship. In

2

2 Thurles, Co. Tipperary – railway station. A pleasant building in the Gothic style (drawing based on the original design by Sancton Wood, architect. The building as erected differs slightly.)

3 Clones, Co. Monaghan, MacCurtain Street – This drawing shows the character and variety of buildings commonly found in the main streets of Irish towns. There are several types of building – shops, big and small; houses; public buildings. The visual expressions are varied. The common denominators are a physical attachment to one another, a general adherence to a building line, and dark pitched roofs. This unity in diversity is an essential characteristic of old European towns but influenced by local conditions.

3

9

towns they are invariably well mannered; in the countryside they fit in with the grain of the landscape. Few may be listed for preservation in a development plan; it would be impossible – indeed undesirable – to preserve them all, but they are still in everyday use, and therefore cannot be considered functionally obsolete as more prestigious buildings often are.

In some instances these local buildings, north and south of the border, have about them an Irishness which makes them part of a common heritage that transcends the political divide. The principal aim of this book is to make the public aware of the ordinary building, and we hope that the study of local architecture will also provide useful lessons for architects and designers, and will perhaps result in distinctive local architecture in modern buildings. This, however, should not mean a mindless imitation of past styles without any real appreciation of their essential purpose and character as is too often seen today, particularly in neo-Georgian housing. The book deals mainly with the external appearance of buildings – the design, style, materials and craftsmanship – with the influence of prevailing architectural theories on them and with their relationship to other buildings or to the landscape. Each building type is treated in outline and its general architectural qualities are discussed briefly. We are conscious, however, that many building types are worthy of greater study. Other institutions and individuals have greater knowledge and infinitely better resources to tackle such subjects in the depth they deserve. It is hoped, however, that this study will also act as an encouragement to further work.

Buildings erected during the last two decades are not, for a number of reasons, examined in detail. Although more ordinary buildings have been erected in recent years than perhaps at any other period, the extent of poor-quality architecture is depressing. There is still architecture of originality and merit being built, which, no doubt, will form part of our heritage in future years, but it is increasingly hard to find. In addition, modern buildings are now so diverse in type, requirements and location, that they are difficult to examine along clearly established lines. For example rural buildings are no longer mainly farms and there are no easily understood differences in style and construction between, say, churches, schools and factories. In any case, it is still too soon to evaluate modern developments fully. This is perhaps best left for another day. Occasionally comments are made on current trends, but principally to draw attention to developments which, in our opinion, are eroding the qualities of local architecture.

Some building types are common to town and country, but this book is concerned primarily with the wide range of building types to be found in towns and villages, as country buildings deserve a study of their own. This book examines streets and squares which were designed and built as an architectural unit and also the individual buildings – houses, shops, churches and schools – that are found in every town.

Many fine examples of local architecture have not been designed by architects, yet they have a quality and character often lacking in present-day buildings, including some which have been professionally designed. If we can discover reasons for the success of the one and the failure of the other, then perhaps we may be able to establish criteria to improve the quality of future buildings. The need for new buildings of all sorts will continue. As in the past, the majority of buildings will be ordinary, everyday types. Surely we must try to achieve as good a standard of design and craftsmanship as did our predecessors, while at the same time meeting present-day requirements.

Chapter Two

The Development of Towns

Ireland has a different urban tradition from other European countries. Geographically isolated, it was not influenced by Roman civilisation, nor was it situated on the great trade and religious routes of medieval Europe. Architecturally, therefore, the process of urban development in Ireland does not follow the mainstream of medieval urban civilisation. However, this does not mean that there are no towns of great antiquity.

A number of cities and towns were founded by the Vikings, and so are at least a thousand years old. All these earlier settlements are on the coastline or major estuaries. This is to be expected on an island which was urbanised from the outside rather than as a process of internal development. The Normans, who arrived towards the end of the twelfth century, built on the earlier Viking foundations. The number of specifically Norman towns is probably small, but includes Carrickfergus, Trim, Athenry and Kilkenny. The Normans established religious foundations, developed markets and generally gave the towns an administrative and commercial basis.

For many centuries, however, the country was in a relatively unsettled state, which culminated in the wars and rebellions of the sixteenth and seventeenth centuries. As in other European countries, the ordinary buildings would have been constructed with timber and wattle. As a result, few fragments of medieval town buildings remain, and practically nothing of domestic architecture. As far as we are concerned, therefore, urban development did not commence on any significant scale until the seventeenth century with the founding of the Ulster Plantation towns. But even these rather basic urban centres were affected by later disturbances in the seventeenth century and there are few tangible remains today. Modern urban development began, therefore, in the eighteenth century and continued practically uninterrupted until the middle of the nineteenth century. During that period Dublin in particular had a century of almost continuous building. It was the second city in the kingdom of Britain and Ireland and architecturally among the most graceful cities in Europe. In the provincial towns development commenced somewhat later and the great period, particularly in the smaller towns, was at the beginning of the nineteenth century. Within a period of no more than forty years the physical form and layout of many towns as we know them today was established. It was a tremendous achievement in building and state development, even by today's standards. It was obviously a time of great economic growth and of rapid population increase, particularly in the countryside. Ireland is fortunate that this significant phase of urban development coincided with a period of high standards in design and taste throughout Europe. Architecture, urban design, art and sculpture were all of social importance.

From the mid-nineteenth century onwards, urban development continued, but on a reduced scale. The great concentration of effort was now in Ulster, particularly in the north-east. However, this period has also left an interesting heritage of buildings, large and small, which for many years has been underestimated, but which is now coming to be more widely appreciated. The next great phase of urban development began in the 1960s and has continued ever since. It has changed the appearance not only of the towns but of the countryside also.

What follows is a brief outline of Irish urban development.

The commonly held view about this period was that there were few organised urban settlements in the country. This view, however, is questioned by some historical geographers and historians; R. A. Butlin in *The Development of the Irish Town* (London 1977) suggests that there may have been organised settlements before the arrival of the Vikings.

While recognising that the legally constituted and tenurially different towns of the Norman colonisation constitute an institutional and morphological innovation in Ireland, it is perhaps wrong to suggest that nothing approaching urban status or function had preceded them. The evidence presented above, albeit in a highly conjectural framework, suggests the strong possibility, in addition to the Viking port towns, that some form of central place or proto-urban settlements had developed. Thus the 'imported urbanism only' thesis is inadequate, and needs further critical examination in the light of fresh evidence, for it does not take sufficient cognisance of the effects of social, economic, religious and political changes which were undoubtedly being experienced in the period from the fifth to the twelfth century, and which resulted in the rise of new forms of social organisation and settlement, and, at the other extreme, the demise and redundancy of some features of political and economic organisation which had survived, in all probability, since the Iron Age.

This was the Golden Age, when Ireland was the Island of Saints and Scholars. Symbols of social and economic wealth were the monasteries, schools and religious foundations. The monasteries were not only concerned with prayer, but were also involved in education, social work, farming and the creation of works of art and crafts. It is arguable that the monasteries were physically organised so that there was a formal relation between the various types of buildings within the complex, each with a different architectural appearance. However none of the great religious foundations from that period subsequently became locations for major urban centres. Some developed into

smaller urban centres such as Kells, and Downpatrick, and perhaps certain cities like Armagh and Kilkenny can trace their origins back to this period.

The Vikings developed their settlements initially along the coastline, founding Dublin, Waterford, Limerick and other towns. Until recently we could only guess what a Viking town looked like, but the Wood Quay excavations in Dublin were of importance in unravelling and explaining the beginnings of our urban heritage. It is tragic that these excavations could not have been undertaken in a more encouraging archaeological climate and the site left in such a way as to provide a permanent and historically accurate example of how the early cities were laid out. Perhaps there are still more archaeological items to be discovered in other cities, but as Dublin was the most important Viking settlement it is unlikely that anything as important as the Wood Quay finds will be discovered.

The Normans developed the earlier Viking settlements and also established some new centres, both on the coast and along more important rivers inland. Many of these towns still exist today and have urban traditions going back to medieval times and earlier. There are, however, few physical remains except for individual castles and churches. The few complete domestic medieval buildings remaining, such as Rothe House and Shee Alms House in Kilkenny and the Alms Houses in Youghal, Co. Cork, therefore, are not only architecturally important, but are a valuable social record of these times. As with the earlier Viking period, we can only imagine the atmosphere and character of the medieval buildings with the help of contemporary illustrations. The last medieval timber-framed domestic building in Dublin was demolished at the beginning of the nineteenth century. In Drogheda old medieval cage-houses remained until 1824.

The historical atmosphere of the older towns can still be sensed, however, in the narrow streets and laneways and in the mixture of land uses in the older parts of these towns. The Middle Ages was a period of wars and disturbances and most towns would have been fortified, but apart from the outstanding example of Athenry, Co. Galway, where the medieval town walls are practically intact, and Youghal to a lesser

4

4 Dublin city, Werburgh Street – Demolished in the early nineteenth century, this was the last remaining timber-framed house in Dublin.
5 Bangor, Co. Down, Gray's Hill – substantial terrace of houses with bay windows and plaster details, typical of many seaside resorts.

5

degree, only odd fragments of medieval fortifications remain. Many town walls may have provided building materials for subsequent developments.

There was a thriving network of towns in medieval Ireland and B. J. Graham in *The Development of the Irish Town* listed 172 centres which had a borough charter. There were also centres which had a fair or market. Most were located along the eastern and south-eastern coastline and inland from this generally east of the line from Limerick to Belfast. Graham also mentions that at that time New Ross, Co. Wexford, was the settlement next in importance to Dublin. Most of these medieval centres have developed into well-known towns today, but some did not develop at all or remained very small. For example, there was a medieval borough in County Antrim called Dumnalleys, and another in County Wexford called Carrick-on-Slaney: little evidence of these remains today, at least not above ground. However, there are still a few fragments of buildings to be seen in Clonmines, Co. Wexford, which was also a significant settlement. Although the Plantations of Ulster and the earlier ones in east Munster and Laois and Offaly (King's and Queen's Counties) were largely rural-based, concentrating on improved methods of agriculture and countryside management, they did result in the establishment of towns. Indeed as part of the conditions attached to the transfer of lands in Ulster the development companies were obliged to establish towns and markets. Some towns were established on the sites of earlier settlements or strongholds, while others were on new ground altogether.

Seventeenth-century towns were on a grander scale than medieval ones and were obviously influenced by Renaissance ideas of layout and planning. A particularly imaginative plan was prepared for Bandon, Co. Cork, by John Boyle. It is difficult to establish if it was ever implemented, since present-day buildings in Bandon date mainly from the eighteenth and nineteenth centuries. However, the concept of twin settlements on both sides of the river, so clearly shown on the seventeenth century plan, still remains today, and is one of the interesting characteristics of the town. In Ulster the early seventeenth century towns would have been fortified, but of these fortifications little remains except in Londonderry, where the walls are among the best examples of military architecture in the country. They remain to-

day much as they were when erected during the seventeenth century development of the city. The hostile situation in which the new Planters operated and the later civil disturbances have meant that there are few urban buildings remaining from this period of development. Whatever buildings survived the wars must have been swept away during the subsequent phase of building in the eighteenth century.

Despite the disturbances, it is likely, particularly in the older parts of towns, that present-day buildings contain fragments of medieval structures and architectural details, such as fireplaces and chimneys. There is a reservoir of history, especially in relation to the building methods of domestic architecture, still to be tapped. Unfortunately there is little public appreciation of this and it is disappointing that older buildings which are in historic areas are being demolished without any attempt to record their architectural features. It should be a matter of public policy that all new developments in historic areas should allow for the systematic recording of buildings that are to be demolished.

1700 – 1850

The great thrust of urban building began in the eighteenth century. Initially development was concentrated in Dublin and the larger towns. Later, as the new land-owning class who were the power behind most schemes became more established, the smaller towns were improved and extended. New streets and squares were laid down based on the current classical ideas of architecture and town planning. Fine and graceful houses were erected to act as town dwellings for the country gentry or as homes of substance for the rapidly developing professional and commercial classes. Smaller houses were built for artisans and tradespeople. During this period the housing conditions of the ordinary people were poor indeed – mainly thatched cabins built of mud or stone walls, little better than those in the rural areas.

The landlord was perhaps the most significant figure with regard to urban development in this period. The estate house and demesne were, and still are in some instances, an important part of the physical structure of towns. He laid down the standards and conditions regarding new buildings, street improvements and other

6

6 Clonmines, Co. Wexford – medieval town remains. A church and a few fragments of buildings are all that remain of the medieval town of Clonmines. It was an important early Norman settlement but never developed as other such settlements did.

7 Athenry, Co. Galway – town walls. Athenry has the best-preserved medieval town walls in Ireland. They can be seen from many approach roads (see map) – views which must have changed little over the centuries. The walls date from about A.D. 1310.

8 Kilkenny city, off Parliament Street – the remnants of a fifteenth-century building; its medieval character and construction can be clearly observed.

7

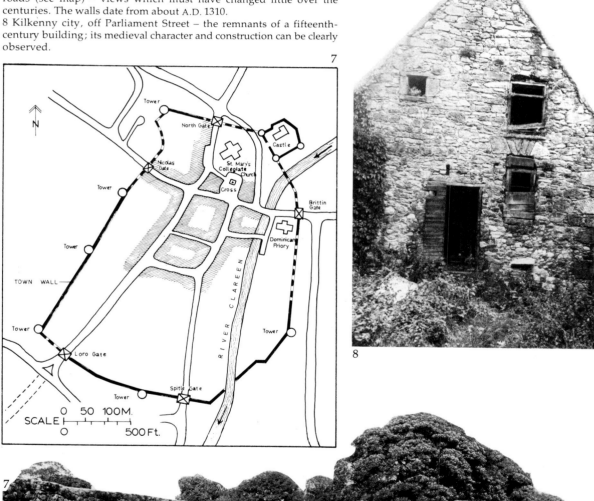

8

7

9

9 Carrick-on-Shannon, Co. Leitrim, Main Street – small shop and dwelling house, similar to thousands throughout the country. This type of building fits snugly into the streetscapes of both small villages and large towns. Its details, such as the doorway, are local adaptations of the grand classical style.

10

10 Wexford town, John's Gate Street – artisan town house. The archway provides access to the rear.

matters, all reflecting his tastes and aspirations. There is as yet little research regarding the administrative problems, the day-to-day organisation and management, that went into the development of towns at this time. This is a much neglected part of our social history, which is certainly of current relevance as we are now in another period of urban growth. For example, were the buildings erected by individual owners on plots specially leased from the landlord? Did the landlord himself become financially involved in the building operations? Were they erected by a builder or speculator who subsequently sold them? What were the exact conditions regarding design and construction? Were they individually designed or were the designs taken from a standard pattern book? There is often information regarding the design of individual important buildings, such as court-houses and market-houses, but as yet little in respect of the street houses. During this period many older streets were widened, new urban spaces were created and public buildings were carefully located. The whole physical structure of most Irish towns as they exist today was conceived and laid down as a unit.

1850 – 1900

After the Famine there was a long period of economic stagnation and social decline which generally affected the smaller towns, except those in the north-east. Here the industrial revolution had a significant impact. Belfast and other towns expanded tremendously. During this period Belfast developed south of the old medieval core around High Street, and the Georgian area around Donegall Square, Linenhall Place and May Street. Today, it is still just possible to identify its Georgian face amid the later Victorian additions. At the end of the eighteenth century Belfast was a small city of twenty to thirty thousand inhabitants. It was a cultured city in many ways, and more influenced by the French political thinking of the time than Dublin was. As yet there was no indication of the tremendous and dramatic development which awaited the city in the latter half of the nineteenth century. Development continued at a gradual pace for a period and then it exploded into what was the greatest period of urban expansion that the country had ever seen.

The development of Belfast and other northern towns was caused by a series of events, beginning with the famines in the 1840s, which resulted in widespread upheaval in rural Ireland and led to great migration, principally to America and Britain, but also to Belfast and the north east. This internal migration was mainly from other parts of Ulster and the west of Ireland. Then the American civil war created a tremendous demand for cotton and linen and the business acumen of the northern Irish people, who had witnessed the beginnings of the industrial revolution in Britain, quickly recognised the opportunities made possible by the new industrial technology. The people who flocked to Belfast brought with them their intense political and religious outlooks. In most other European industrial cities the political and religious beliefs of the new migrants were blurred and changed by new attitudes brought about by urban conditions. The reverse seems to have happened in Belfast and the political and religious divisions were sharpened by the effects of urban development. Even today, the conflicting cultures of Gael and Planters have yet to come to terms with each other in the small nineteenth century Belfast streets.

Elsewhere, in the larger cities and provincial towns, development continued, but at a much slower pace, and only in Dublin, and to a lesser extent in Cork, were there any major new developments such as street buildings and city extensions. Architectural styles and fashions had also changed significantly. A feature of the period was the growing concern for social and public health, which resulted in many new types of public buildings and housing for the ordinary workers and artisans. The Gothic revival, popular from the mid-nineteenth century onwards, was the most commonly accepted architectural style for public buildings, especially churches. The change of style was less noticeable in domestic buildings. It is not uncommon to find classically inspired domestic architecture from the late nineteenth century. The improvement in transportation, particularly the railways, influenced urban development and increased the availability of building materials. A common feature of many late nineteenth-century developments, especially in smaller towns, is the use of brick instead of stone.

The development of the railways gave a new impetus to traditional watering places such as Bray, Co. Wicklow, and Bangor, Co. Down. There was a distinctive style of architecture associated with resort development throughout Europe, Regency/Italianate, based generally on the appearance of Italian Renaissance palaces, with widespread use of plaster as a finish, often with intricate and impressive architectural details. Many commercial premises which were improved at this time adopted the same style and highly ornamental facades are a feature in a number of provincial towns in Ireland. This development is particularly exemplified by fine residential terraces in Dun Laoghaire, Bangor, Portrush and other places.

1900 – 1960

The slow pace of urban development continued. Many public buildings were erected, principally at the beginning of the century following the establishment of the new County and Urban District Councils. There was still public concern with social and community matters, particularly housing, and later health and industrial development. This period, however, was affected by the two world wars, the 'Troubles', and the problems of the depression. Architectural styles generally responded to current tastes and fashions. The Gothic was becoming less fashionable; more common was the new 'arts and crafts' style. The 'modern' style began to be used during the thirties and forties. However the classical style was always popular and it is not uncommon to find small terraces of houses which have an early nineteenth-century look, but which on investigation turn out to have been built around the turn of this century.

Offices, as a special building type, became more common, and were the precursors of a life-style which is greatly changing the shapes of cities and towns today.

From 1920 onwards different administrative and political systems influenced architecture both north and south of the border, although initially actual styles and designs did not change all that much. However, no longer would the same standard Board of Works school be erected in Down, Donegal, Antrim or Cork. Northern Ireland, as part of a stronger economy, had more money to expend on building than the newly formed Irish Free State. The immediate post-war years witnessed major housing programmes, principally in the area of public rather than private housing. This was also a period of continuous population decline, particularly in southern Ireland, not a suitable atmos-

phere for the creation of interesting architecture. However, many of the buildings erected in this period are of significance, not least those in housing.

1960 TO THE PRESENT

Ireland is now experiencing another phase in urban development, which in many ways mirrors the late eighteenth and early nineteenth centuries, as it is influenced by broadly similar economic and demographic changes. In the Republic the population is increasing dramatically and emigration is no longer a soft option for Ireland either north or south. Proportionally the Republic has the youngest population in western Europe. It is estimated that it will have over four million people by the year 2000. At that time, the population of the entire island could be approaching six million. If the figures are projected forward to the year 2030, a mere fifty years away and a short time in the life-span of any country, the total population on the island could be approaching eight million people. The last time the population of Ireland approached eight million was in the 1830s before the Great Famine. Is history repeating itself after two hundred years?

Northern Ireland has, however, experienced a decade of trouble, as a result of which many fine streets and individual buildings have been destroyed. Here, in addition to an increased population to cope with, there will be a need to rebuild damaged town centres.

It is likely and desirable that economic and social growth will continue in some form or other, although not necessarily in the same way as in recent years. Growth is dependent on, among other factors, the provision of energy, but the days of an unlimited supply of cheap energy are gone. It seems likely not only that the need for energy conservation will compel us to make the best use of existing resources but that there will be a movement towards more compact urban settlement patterns, rather than the urban sprawl that cheap petrol gave rise to in the sixties and early seventies. In the previous period of rapid population expansion the pressures were felt mainly in the countryside. However, despite modern changes in the countryside it does appear that from now on the major emphasis of physical development will be in existing settlements. It is also probable that the existing towns will

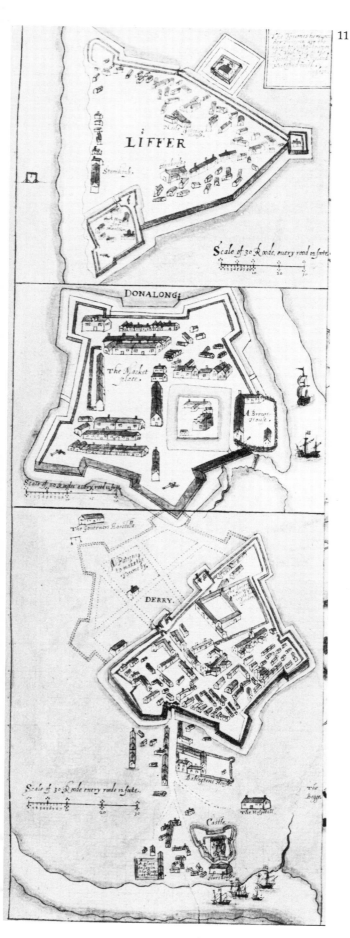

11

12

11 Ulster Plantation – contemporary map showing plans of some Ulster Plantation towns.

12 Youghal, Co. Cork, North Main Street – These alms houses are among the few complete seventeenth-century urban domestic buildings to be found in the country.

13 Tramore, Co. Waterford, Main Street – street-houses of pleasing proportions. The archway forms an important visual link and allows good access to the rear.

14 Newcastle West, Co. Limerick, Maiden Street – old town house. Possibly a late medieval cabin in an urban setting. The iron roof is laid on old thatch. Buildings such as this may be anything from one hundred to three hundred years old.

13

14

expand as much in the next twenty years as they have over the last two hundred (see my *The Irish Town*, Dublin 1975).

It is an opportune time, therefore, to examine the architecture of our towns and villages. This is where the great mass of buildings and the bulk of our architectural heritage are located. Theoretically there should be little to worry about. There is now comprehensive planning legislation designed specifically to control and direct future development and to protect the architectural quality of the places where we live. But it is now widely appreciated that legislation alone solves few problems. A preservation order can be made on a building, but unless some effort is made to maintain the building and the necessary finance is available the formal act of preservation may achieve little. It is both undesirable and impossible to preserve the great majority of buildings. They are ordinary, everyday buildings in continuous use and have often been adapted to suit changing needs and conditions.

In small towns there may be few individual buildings of great architectural or historical importance. In assessing the character of a town it is often a street or square viewed as a whole that is the crucial factor. In this regard ordinary buildings are equally, if not more, relevant. The court-house in Carlow, for example, is architecturally one of the most impressive public buildings in provincial Ireland. It has an important setting at the junction of two quite pleasant streets and rightly it is listed for preservation in the local development plan. But if the buildings in the adjacent streets were replaced by unsympathetic new structures the preservation of the individual building would be meaningless. Another example is Hillsborough, Co. Down, architecturally one of the most significant towns in the country with an impressive array of buildings of good individual quality. However, the character of this charming town is created not just by these important buildings, but by total settings, the relation of the buildings to the space in which they are located and, most importantly, the way the ordinary buildings in the town relate to the grander ones. It is this total concept which is Hillsborough's most important quality, and rightly the entire town centre has been declared a conservation area.

The essence of urban architecture is that you rarely see a building in isolation, as for example in a parkland or rural setting. A street may consist of a variety of houses, perhaps two-storey and single-storey, with plastered fronts and slated roofs. The windows may be pleasantly proportioned, and there is a satisfying composition about the group. Imagine one of the group destroyed by fire and replaced by a flat-roofed structure with large windows: at a stroke the unity of the street is destroyed, and irrespective of the standard of work and its functional requirements, its identity is severely damaged. Unfortunately we are not talking in theoretical terms: there are all too many examples of such insensitive development throughout the country. It is only by focusing attention on what makes up their individual social, historical and architectural qualities and their role in the overall character of the street that the full significance of ordinary buildings can be appreciated.

If changes are required let us hope they will be made with a sense of good neighbourliness regarding other buildings and an appreciation of the buildings' own qualities. In any town there are different types of buildings, from the church, always an important public building, to the corner shop on the side street. There are expressions of the multi-purpose functions of towns, for example living, commerce, industry, religion, education, health, recreation and death. They reflect social and historical traditions and they express the architectural tastes and standards of craftsmanship achieved by previous generations. But time does not stand still. Buildings may become obsolete for present uses, although remaining structurally sound. There is a challenge in adapting them to new uses while respecting their character. Where they are of social significance there is always a better chance of this happening, since the community as a body may be concerned. The fate of the ordinary building, however, is at the mercy of the knowledge, appreciation and sensitivity of its owner.

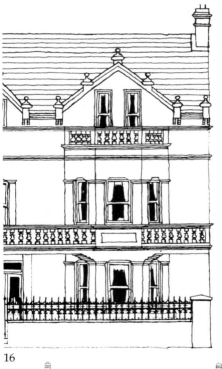

15 Carlow town, Dublin Road – This street provides an appropriate setting for Carlow Court-house. Ill-conceived changes would take from the architectural qualities of the court-house.

17 Dun Laoghaire, Co. Dublin, Marine Road – Town Hall. A fine example of municipal buildings from the late nineteenth century.

17

16 Bundoran, Co. Donegal, Bay View Terrace – These houses were built in the Gothic style with high roofs and bay windows. They differed in style from earlier houses although the accommodation was often the same.

16

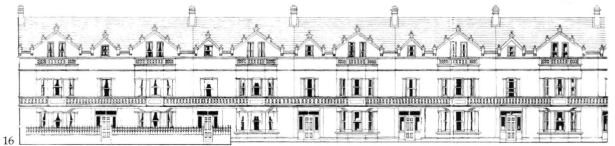

16

Chapter Three

The Structure of Towns

The layout and total physical structure of a town is fundamental to its character, but this is not easy for the lay person to comprehend. A town cannot be viewed like an individual building, a piece of sculpture or a painting, whose essential qualities can often be perceived from a single viewpoint. It is true that a view of a town from a nearby hill or from the air may give a clear picture of its overall character, but this is only an introduction, and towns can best be understood by walking through them. Every town has its individual character. Its form and shape are influenced by its original function, the topography in which it is situated and the architectural style and characteristics of its buildings. Its history has also influenced its present-day character. The spaciousness of the eighteenth-century town is in striking contrast to the physical complexities of towns whose medieval foundations are obvious, though the buildings in the central area of both types of town will usually date from the same period, the early nineteenth century. The atmosphere and appearance of Ennis, Co. Clare, is in marked contrast to Cookstown, Co. Tyrone; the layout of Dromore, Co. Down, contrasts sharply with its neighbour Castlewellan; the narrow streets of Athenry are in contrast to the wide streets and square of Gort, also in County Galway. Beragh, Co. Tyrone, is the quintessence of a small town, with its small-scale buildings arranged on either side of the single street. Galbally, Co. Limerick, is another small town with roughly the same population, providing a similar level of services, but in this instance the buildings are grouped around a central open space.

Much of the charm of smaller towns lies in the differences to be found among them, but on the other hand there are broad general characteristics which many towns share. There are those towns which consist of little more than a single street, while in other towns the streets are at right angles and parallel to the main street, on a rectangular pattern. Elsewhere the main feature is a central square with streets radiating out of it. Settlements which were newly established during the seventeenth century and substantially improved in the early nineteenth century generally have a clearly defined physical pattern. The smaller settlements usually have one central space, a little street or square, with the buildings grouped around it. As towns become bigger the layout is obviously more complex, but the basic pattern of streets and squares is repeated, all on a formal pattern. Occasionally the older medieval patterns were not disturbed and the new buildings respected the street lines and rights-of-way laid down earlier. Towns like Wexford, Ennis, and Kinsale have retained their medieval layout to a marked degree. In other towns, notably Armagh and Limerick, the medieval and classical street styles exist side by side.

As a general rule, eighteenth-century developments catered for the new professional and commercial classes, whose businesses and residences were located in newly developed streets. This has given rise to the so called 'Irish' and 'English' towns, as older and newer areas, respectively, of the same town were called. The 'Irish town' is more informal in layout with narrow, winding streets and smaller buildings. Sometimes the name 'Irish town' as well as the medieval atmosphere is retained, as in Dublin and

18

18 Cookstown, Co. Tyrone; Ennis, Co. Clare – These photographs illustrate the contrast between the rigid linear form of Cookstown, planned and developed as a complete entity, and Ennis, where the modern layout is influenced by the medieval foundations.

19 Dublin city, Merrion Square – street layout. This map, prepared by Jonathan Barker – an important eighteenth-century surveyor – illustrates the manner in which Georgian Dublin, and indeed many other towns in Ireland, were laid out and developed in the eighteenth century. It is among the first town-planning maps. The building plots were leased out with strict control over design and materials.

18

19

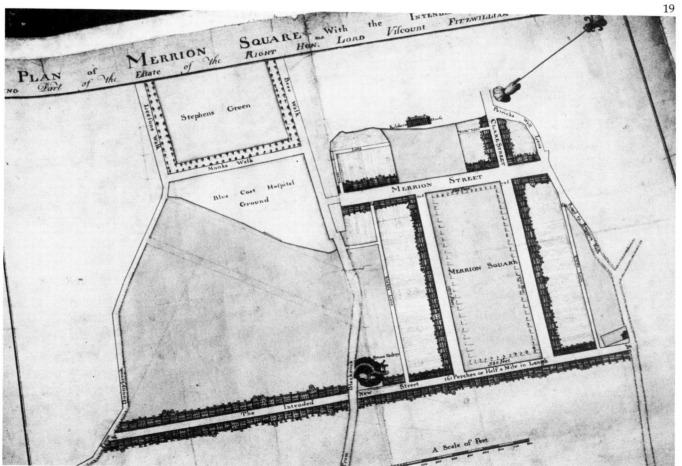

Kilkenny. These older areas were less disturbed during the first phase of modern development. At the beginning of this century – judging from old photographs – they still contained interesting old buildings. It is likely that in these areas there are fragments of craftsmanship dating back to medieval times. Urban archaeology has until recently been neglected and there is much work to be carried out. The origins and development of any town are always worth studying.

STREETS AND SQUARES

From the beginnings of urban civilisation the most common element in towns is the street or square. Essentially a street is defined as a grouping of buildings which face on to a public thoroughfare; usually the buildings are physically connected to each other and may be similar but with minor variations, as in the Georgian streets and squares. On the other hand, they may be different in size, design, shape and use, as in the older medieval settlements and in many small towns today. The common link is the street itself, the public thoroughfare, where all the major communal activities take place. In medieval times the street was usually a narrow path suitable only for pedestrians and small wheeled vehicles. In the Renaissance and Georgian periods, the street became a symbol of power and majesty and often its scale dominated the nearby buildings. However, it is the physical attachment of one building to another which is the principal characteristic of older streets of all periods, and this has been a major feature of urban aesthetics.

In addition to being an aesthetic element the street is also important to the social life of a community. Street games and street names are part of the folklore and culture of town living. Games like hopscotch, maypole and street football were of such importance that even if the ball was only made of paper, the competition and excitement were no less to the players concerned than in a great national fixture. These were the glorious days of the street, when children could play from morning till night without causing anxiety to their parents. These were also the days before the motor car, which, despite its advantages as a means of transport, has brought only danger and pollution to the traditional street.

Street names are also important, whether they commemorate a local dignitary or an important event or refer to the original activities in the street. We may come across a Tailors' Row now without tailors, a Mill Street, where all traces of the mill are gone, a Fair Green, where the fairs are only a memory for older people. The street was a place where all the action was and walking the main street was a very popular pastime a mere generation ago.

The street is essentially of linear proportions but the square is a broad space where the street in effect becomes wider to provide more room for an important activity, for example, a market or the celebration of a great person or event. The square as an urban space has always been considered prestigious and many of the fine urban spaces throughout the world are squares in some form or other. Important movements in history originated in cities and the seeds of such movements often germinated in the great communal activities attracted to the central square.

It can be argued that one of Dublin's great drawbacks is the lack of a central space which could become the focus of community activity. College Green has some potential in this regard, but at the moment it is merely a traffic junction. Despite all the concern with urban planning in recent years, there is as yet no specific proposal to provide the capital city with a new public space where the ordinary citizen would have precedence over traffic. Belfast is luckier, as Donegall Square provides a natural focus in the heart of the city. Any town or village which has a central space can count itself lucky, and every effort should be made to ensure that it becomes a genuine focus of communal activity. Measures such as paving and planting and restricting the intensity of traffic can achieve considerable improvements for a relatively small cost.

The relationship between streets and squares is an important aspect of the way in which towns function aesthetically. The contrast between the narrowness and linearity of the street and the spaciousness of the square always adds interest to any town. Street architecture is one of the most delightful aspects of our architectural heritage. It is not uncommon to find shops, public buildings, banks and houses, some large, some quite small, strung together along a street like beads on a necklace, often different in specific details, but relating to each other principally from the very fact of physical contact, but also through a consistent

20 Birr Co. Offaly, Oxmantown Mall – This street is a complete unit with the church at one end and the castle entrance at the other. The unity of space and the quality of the individual buildings are important aspects of the street.

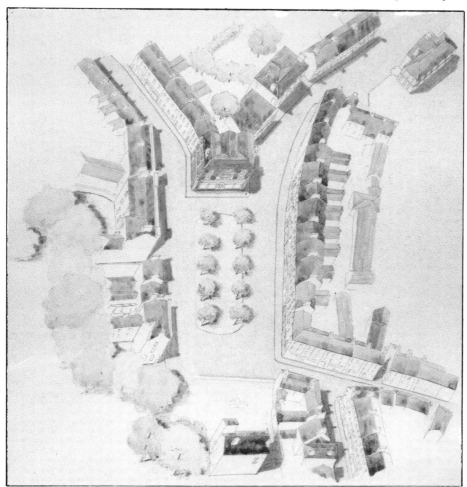

21 Newcastle West, Co. Limerick – A bird's-eye view emphasises the essential physical structure of a town. This understanding is particularly important for planners, architects and all involved in the development of towns. Every school should have such an illustration or aerial photograph – it could be of considerable help in promoting a greater knowledge of the local town.

rhythm of windows, doors, roofs, and a broad similarity of building materials. In the smaller villages and towns the use and function can change from building to building, but still the overall effect is pleasing. In the larger towns, uses are more uniform. There are streets consisting mainly of shops and commercial premises and streets which consist mainly of houses. Here again, there may be variation in size and subtle changes in design. In any assessment of urban design the concept of the street and square should always be considered in totality. It is possible to destroy the entire uniformity, character and cohesion of a street by the insertion of one insensitively designed building. Sometimes damage can be caused simply by changing the proportions and design of windows, insignificant as that may appear in relation to a single house.

The traditional building plot reflects the importance of the street as a social and economic unit. It is long and narrow, usually twenty to thirty feet wide. Wider plots are unusual and belong mainly to public buildings or may be a result of the amalgamation of adjacent properties. Narrow frontages allow the maximum number of properties to face onto the street. The entrance to the rear of the premises is often through an archway under the buildings, which in itself creates an attractive feature in many street scenes. At present many back gardens lie idle and under-used, the rich soil growing nothing but a variety of weeds. They often contain attractive stone outbuildings usually falling into neglect and disrepair. These fallow areas represent a great unused land resource of architectural potential and there are many opportunities to create new streets and urban spaces(see also *The Irish Town*).

In recent years there has been a decline in the aesthetic quality and social importance of the street as an integral part of the urban fabric, for several reasons, principally the growth of motor traffic. Many streets, previously safe and pleasant places to move about in, have become noisy and dangerous. The widespread use of the motor car led to the development of a philosophy that the street was no longer a place for community activity or residential use, but purely an artery which was to be shaped and designed to suit the needs of traffic. Existing streets were widened purely to facilitate the movement of traffic, not to create new urban spaces. In the smaller towns this traffic is mostly only passing through, so its increased speed is a source of danger to the residents and of damage to the buildings, and it brings few economic benefits. Many other streets declined economically and socially, not because they were actually widened, but because it was indicated on plans that a road-widening scheme might be contemplated in the future. Of course there is nothing intrinsically wrong with street improvements if they form part of a comprehensive plan of urban renewal and provide for newly designed streets with adequate living and social accommodation.

Another reason for the decline of the street is essentially aesthetic and social. One of the significant facts of town development in the past was the physical attachment of one building to another whether in the medieval street or in the later and more formal streets and squares. In previous periods of urban improvement, the terrace was an acceptable building form wholly consistent with the physical and philosophical concept of the town. The villa in its own parkland was essentially a rural style, influenced initially by Palladian ideas. In the late nineteenth century the development of the large detached house in the suburbs introduced the concept of the country villa in an urban setting, but at that time it was not widespread and was limited to the cities and major provincial towns. Usually there was also sufficient land to allow the creation of a unified and pleasant environment between house and grounds. Nevertheless, the terrace was commonly used until the 1920s, particularly for residential buildings. Transport was still limited, moving along direct routes by railway or tramcar, and obviously there was still no great social stigma attached to the idea of joining one building to another. However, the detached house had begun to assume an aura of grandeur.

In the 1930s the growing use of the motor car widened locational choices and the detached and semi-detached house became the popular urban form. It has continued ever since, reaching extreme and perhaps absurd limits where bungalows are built in town centres. The terrace, a unified building concept, was suddenly unfashionable and unacceptable. It was associated with lower income and poor quality houses. There was little awareness that in the past the whole spectrum of society, from the very wealthy to the ordinary worker, saw nothing wrong with living in a terraced development.

Today in expensive housing estates the

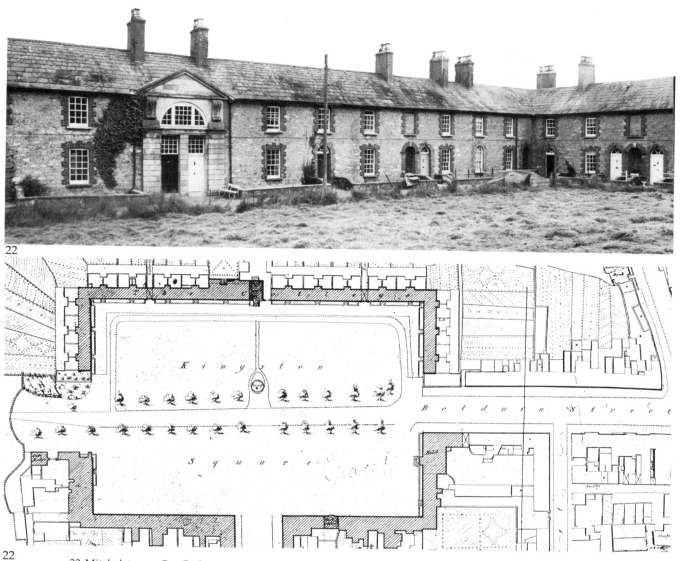

22

22 Mitchelstown, Co. Cork – Kingston Square, one of the finest eighteenth-century spaces in Ireland with its architectural characteristics still largely intact.

23

24

23 Bantry, Co. Cork, New Street – The graceful vertical rhythms of these facades, particularly the upper storeys, are part of the charm of this street as of most old streets. A wrongly proportioned building here would, at a stroke, destroy this essential quality.

24 Mountmellick, Co. Laois, O'Connell Square – The art of creating pleasant spaces by turning buildings at right angles to each other is rarely practised today.

builders have carried this new concept to extremes. So-called detached houses are built with no more than a foot or two between each house and the entire building plot may be tiny. This is a far cry from the grandiose concepts of eighteenth-century villas, or even the early detached houses of the 1930s. It is also a sad and crude alternative to the fine residential streets in town centres. The concept of the physically integrated residential street is gone and is replaced by the idea of the villa, which can be aesthetically successful on large sites, but never on the small plots common today.

Social attitudes and conditions, of course, influence architecture. It is no longer feasible to build three- and four-storey houses with servant-quarters in the basement or upper floors. The modern house needs to provide only for the immediate requirements of the family. The dictates of the motor car, moving or parked, influence the design of houses and the layout of housing areas, but these are difficulties that imaginative design can overcome. The real problem is that a total philosophy of design has not yet been worked out for the suburb. The importance of layout and the need to utilise the existing topography and landscape are rarely taken into account. Most suburban areas are developed without any conscious design ethic and conform to a rag-bag of planning regulations which have no basic design concept and rarely relate to a particular site.

Even in new commercial and community developments the individually isolated building is widespread. A town-centre plan for a new area consists of individual buildings located without relationship to each other. They are usually separated off in a self-important but utterly boring fashion, the antithesis of the medieval market place or the nineteenth-century square. Uses are rigidly segregated wherever possible. In medium-sized towns new commercial developments are commonly single-storey, single-purpose schemes.

Some years ago, it was likely that the concept of the traditional street or square would disappear altogether. Few new urban spaces were being created and most existing streets and urban spaces were gradually being whittled away, except for a few which would then be moth-balled in splendid but lonely isolation. Lately however, there have been encouraging signs that the decline in the quality of our existing streets and urban spaces may be reversed, or at least halted. Amenity societies, residents' associations and private individuals fought back against what designers and developers were doing to the streets of their local towns. The energy crisis has emphasised the advantages of living in existing centres, particularly when commuting costs are increasing daily. The merits and qualities of the older streets and spaces are being rediscovered. The apparent disadvantages of living over a shop are balanced by the fact that a person may live closer to their work, and certainly closer to existing facilities, to shops, libraries, churches and schools. This has benefits for people of all ages and occupations and not just the young and trendy. For instance, the terrace allows greater energy savings than detached houses. New streets, on traditional lines but with modern amenities, are being designed again, for example Dean Street in the cathedral quarter of Kilkenny.

In certain older areas streets committees have been formed to protect the existing amenities, particularly from the effects of through-traffic or day-long parking. There will, however, be a need to design for new standards and conditions. The urban street of today has to cater for a different society from the street of the past, but there is much to be learned from an understanding of the design and techniques used by earlier generations of town builders.

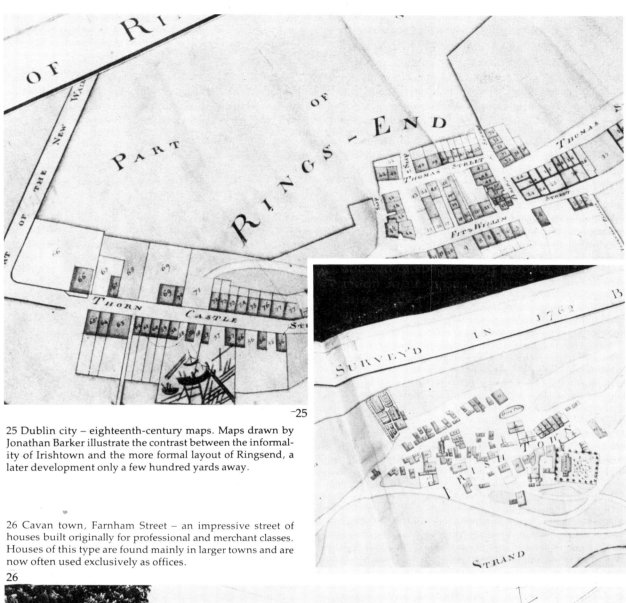

—25

25 Dublin city – eighteenth-century maps. Maps drawn by Jonathan Barker illustrate the contrast between the informality of Irishtown and the more formal layout of Ringsend, a later development only a few hundred yards away.

26 Cavan town, Farnham Street – an impressive street of houses built originally for professional and merchant classes. Houses of this type are found mainly in larger towns and are now often used exclusively as offices.

26

Chapter Four

Houses

The commonest town building is the house. Houses are of different types: there are large houses in spacious grounds, substantial three- and four-storey town houses, entire streets consisting mainly of two-storey houses, suburbs of detached and semi-detached houses and, not least, humble cottages. Their life-span usually exceeds that of the families who first occupied them. They are subject to changes which can sometimes enhance the architectural character of the building and improve its structural condition. But more frequently the opposite is the case: houses commonly decline because of lack of maintenance or change of use, such as conversion into offices, though this need not necessarily lower maintenance standards. Decline may also be due to intensification of use, whereby houses originally built for one family are used as multi-apartment buildings.

The house, more than any other building type still remains a universal and basic unit. Houses continue to be built in various locations and to different designs. Living requirements have changed, but the concept of the family unit is generally as relevant now as it was in Georgian or medieval times. Other traditional building types have gone out of fashion or have changed out of all recognition. For example, few market houses or court-houses are now built and a new railway station would be a most unusual development although there are many arguments for increasing investment in the railway system. Buildings such as factories, hospitals and, to a lesser extent, schools have been considerably changed by modern technology and new social requirements.

During the period when the present structures of towns were laid down there was little distinction between place of residence and work – shopkeepers lived over their shops, craftspeople over their workshops, lawyers and doctors in their rooms. This is still the norm in the village or smaller town but it is changing in medium-sized towns and in larger centres. Here it is now exceptional to live and work in the same building.

In Ireland, a house is usually a self-contained building with its own entrance from the street and a private open space at the back, perhaps a small yard or even a substantial garden. There is little tradition, as in some other countries, for apartment dwellings, although in recent years apartment blocks are being built in the cities. No doubt this trend will continue because of changing social attitudes. The tenement dwellings in Dublin and other larger towns are an exception to the preference for individual dwelling houses rather than apartment living, but they were brought about by appalling social and economic conditions: they were in essence a last refuge rather than a first choice.

Housing has always been the subject of community concern. There is probably more legislation dealing with housing than with other building types. This is understandable since the house is fundamentally a shelter within which an acceptable environment for a family unit can be created. The right to shelter is a basic human right, but unfortunately it is not always available: housing crises are not a new phenomenon. Although housing has been influenced by the architectural styles and fashions of the day, its fundamental requirements change less than those of other building types. We will categorise housing types historically and with

27

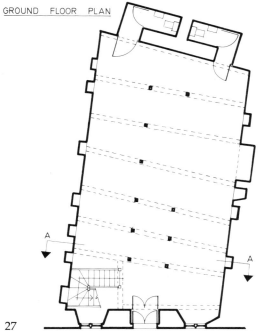

GROUND FLOOR PLAN

A

A

27

SECTION A - A

27

27 Kilkenny city, Rose Inn Street – Shee Alms House. Erected in 1568 by the Shee family as a charitable institution, this is one of the few urban domestic buildings still remaining from the period. It has recently been restored in an architecturally correct manner by Kilkenny Corporation with advice from the Office of Public Works. The original architectural and constructional qualities of the building can now be clearly seen.

28 Carlingford, Co. Louth – the Mint: a medieval town house dating from the fifteenth century, still part of the street pattern.

28

29

FIRST FLOOR LEVEL

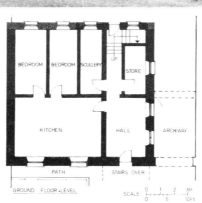

BEDROOM BEDROOM SCULLERY STORE

KITCHEN   HALL   ARCHWAY

PATH   STAIRS OVER

GROUND FLOOR LEVEL

SCALE 0 1 2 3M
       0   5   10Ft

DINING ROOM

LIVING ROOM   ENTRANCE   STUDY
                HALL

PATH

HALL LEVEL

UP

29 Birr, Co. Offaly, St John's Mall – townhouses. A classic prototype of the eighteenth-century townhouse – the two-storey-over-basement house with central hall and staircase. The plan was essentially simple with the dividing walls carried up through the house and a double pile roof, i.e. with a valley in the centre. Such houses were detached or semi-detached, but more usually in a terrace with a skilful use of archways with rooms over. The building sites were long and narrow; access was usually through the front, with coach-house and outbuildings at the rear. This Birr house dates from approximately 1814, and there are many other similar houses in this architecturally important town. The map shows the location and garden space.

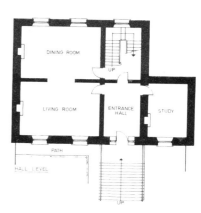

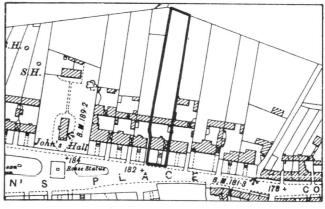

30

30 Moville, Co. Donegal, Quay Street – These houses are no more than cottages
and have a refined architectural style.

31 Carrickart, Co. Donegal, Main Street – This shop and house, although improved
over the years, has retained its character and domestic scale.

reference to the development of towns.

Ireland is unique among European countries in having very few complete medieval urban domestic buildings, although medieval Ireland did have a hierarchy of urban centres not markedly different from that of today. It is remarkable that cities such as Dublin, Waterford or Limerick – all strong medieval centres – have no remaining visible domestic buildings that pre-date 1600. Indeed they have few if any pre-dating 1700. There are, however, fragments of older buildings incorporated in many present-day structures. There are also houses, usually small, with a distinctive character but which have been considerably improved and which may reveal details dating from an earlier period. What are the reasons for this widespread lack of early domestic architecture? The country was in a state of civil unrest for many centuries, but many other countries in Europe were in a similar situation. Perhaps this unrest, in conjunction with a rather poor quality of building materials – wattle and mud rather than stone or timber – is a reason for this lack of medieval remains. Another reason may be the massive rebuilding that took place in the late eighteenth and the nineteenth centuries. This rebuilding may not have been massive by the standards of other countries, but it was enormous in relation to what was already there. It was carried out in a bold spirit and had little respect for existing buildings.

In any case it is likely that even during the mid-nineteenth century many towns may have had reasonably intact medieval houses. Perhaps if they had survived a few more generations they might then have been saved permanently. Where current investigations reveal substantial medieval remains every effort should be made to restore the building to its original form. Such buildings are extremely important, especially as we have so few of them.

Of the few late medieval houses still remaining in Irish towns, Rothe House and the Shee Alms House in Kilkenny have been sensitively restored both architecturally and historically. The Alms Houses in Youghal, however, are in a ruinous state and unless restoration is commenced soon it may be too late. Of these buildings, only Rothe House is a residential dwelling in the usual sense: the others are community buildings of one

sort or another. Some medieval castles and tower houses are still standing, but these were built by the aristocracy and so fall outside our category of local architecture. They were built of stone and roofed with thatch or slate.

The ordinary domestic buildings of this period, particularly the earlier ones, would probably have been built of mud and wattle with roofs made of thatch or perhaps only of grass sods. It can be assumed that these buildings would have been broadly similar to countryside cottages, ranging from quite commodious dwellings subdivided into rooms to the more basic type where humans and animals were accommodated within the same internal space.

This period was the most important phase of urban development to date, and so the houses from this time constitute a significant part of our domestic architectural heritage. Such houses are usually found in the centres of larger towns. In smaller towns and villages they may still constitute the bulk of housing. They vary in size and type from the large mansion in its own grounds, obviously modelled on the great houses in the countryside, to the small single-storey cabin similar in plan form and constructional details to the traditional cottage of the countryside. In rare cases these smaller houses are sometimes still thatched. The majority of residential buildings from this period, however, consist of terraced houses of two to three storeys and occasionally four storeys which were built along the major streets of towns. In medium-sized towns these houses are often interspersed with shops and other buildings. In larger towns there are impressive streets of eighteenth- and early nineteenth-century houses comparable to the best in the cities. The type of house and its style often reflected the social standing of the occupiers. More prosperous merchants and professional classes lived in substantial three- to four-storey houses, smaller shopkeepers more often than not lived over their shop, artisans and clerks lived in two-storey buildings and ordinary workers and labourers in single-storey cottages, usually on the outskirts of smaller towns and in clearly defined areas in larger centres.

One of the most interesting aspects of domestic architecture from this period is its widespread distribution throughout the

32 Nenagh, Co. Tipperary, Ormond street – These small houses are likely to be quite old. They may originally have been single-storey and thatched.
34 Drogheda, Co. Louth – An illustration showing the last recorded timber-framed urban houses in Ireland. This house was on the corner of Shop Street and Laurence Street but was demolished in 1824.

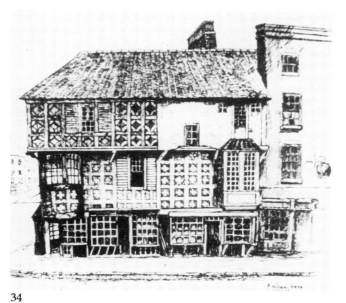

34

33 Limerick city, off Nicholas Street – These small cottages, adjacent to St Mary's Cathedral, may well contain medieval fragments – certainly the laneways are likely to have existed for a long time.

33

35 Gorey, Co. Wexford, Ferns Road – Thatched cabins are located on the outskirts of many towns. They may have been constructed on earlier foundations. The remnants of such cottages can still be seen today, the thatch being replaced by slate or the buildings raised to two storeys. Such buildings may be more important historically than their owners realise.

35

36 Abbeyfeale, Co. Limerick, Main Street – elaborate plasterwork on a small street-house, perhaps by Pat McAuliffe or a local tradesman influenced by his work.

36

37 Youghal, Co. Cork, North Main Street – a nineteenth-century shop-house, now exclusively a dwelling, but with its fine architectural qualities retained.

37

38

38 Castleblayney, Co. Monaghan, Carrickmacross Road – Alms houses. These houses were erected by a charitable trust. Of high architectural character with very good brick detailing, they are still being used for their original purpose.

39

39 Birr, Co. Offaly, Eden Road – small estate houses with a charm and quality associated with such developments. They have changed little over the years.

country. Even quite small towns may contain examples of all types. Architecturally their great characteristics are simplicity of design and construction. They were classical in style, usually with a local flavour to the architectural details and materials used. This common architectural expression has certainly created a sense of uniformity throughout the country. To the casual observer, town houses of this period may appear the same in most towns, but when examined in detail they reveal many local variations in architectural details, constructional methods, plot sizes and other matters.

Walls were usually constructed of stone and covered with lime plaster. Brick was not widely used except in the cities, as it was available only in major ports, but stone was plentiful throughout the country. Timber was used for floors and roofing. The roof coverings were usually slates, particularly in larger houses. Initially many smaller cabins would have been thatched and indeed many two-storey houses may originally have been covered with thatch. Elevational treatment was generally restrained and severe; the more elaborate plasterwork was to come later. The main focus of attention was usually the doorway. Here, even in small houses, pleasant classical details such as elegant Doric or Ionic columns constructed in timber or stone and delicate iron fanlights were used. Larger houses had more elaborate, elegant and impressive details.

Over the years many changes have been made to these houses: lime plaster has given way to cement plaster applied either smooth and painted or rough cast; the twelve-pane Georgian windows have been replaced by two-pane types; cottages have exchanged the thatched roof for slates. These changes are not always an improvement aesthetically, but they reflect different building methods and improved social and economic circumstances.

In recent years more drastic changes have occurred, particularly through the use of the standard modern window which is horizontal in proportion in contrast to the vertical lines of the classical window. It has been used widely with unsatisfactory effects. One interesting change has been a change of use from shop to residential building. In some streets nearly all the original buildings would have been shops. Today shopping has been affected by the trend towards larger units, as a result of which small shops are closing. The shop becomes a living room, but when the traditional shopfront is retained it adds charm and interest. This is particularly a feature of towns in the south-west.

Larger and medium-sized houses were frequently built on previously undeveloped land, or existing structures were removed to make way for them. Smaller houses, often single-storey, are essentially different. The building of houses for the poorer classes on a wide scale did not take place to any great extent until the latter part of the nineteenth century. These urban cottages have quite a varied history and are among the oldest structures in towns – many may pre-date 1700. They have undergone much change and improvement over the years. The thatch has been replaced by slates or galvanised iron and some have been increased from single- to two-storey. Their plot sizes vary from small yards in some places to large gardens. Large gardens are found particularly in smaller towns where these houses were on the outskirts. The architectural quality of small houses, which occasionally create a rural atmosphere in an urban setting, is too often underestimated. Some still lack modern amenities, but with relatively little expense they could be transformed into attractive and distinctive homes.

1850 – 1920

During this period the pace of urban development in small and medium-sized towns slowed down considerably, except in the north-east and in seaside towns. In the smaller settlements, whose fortunes were closely linked with those of the countryside, development practically stopped. In the larger towns and cities, housing development continued but in a different social and architectural climate. It was a time of greater social concern, particularly about living conditions in urban areas, and this was the impetus behind significant housing developments.

Architectural fashions had also changed and the simplicity of classical design in universal use now gave way to more ornate and diverse architectural expressions, which were at first influenced by the Gothic, interpreted in a variety of ways, and later by formal Italianate styles, by the picturesque arts and crafts movement, the quaintness of mock Tudor and the exciting expressions of Art Nouveau. The improvement of methods of transport meant that building materials previously uncommon in certain districts were now more widely used.

40

41

42

40 Dublin city, Southview Terrace, South Circular Road – This group of houses, built towards the end of the nineteenth century, shows the influence of the Tudor revival with gable fronts, projecting upper floors and black and white timbering.

41 Tralee, Co. Kerry, Day Square – typical early nineteenth-century houses, all with distinctive expressions but in the classical style. They form a significant part of the local architectural heritage.

42 Holywood, Co. Down, Ulster Folk Museum – a group of nineteenth-century industrial houses which were transferred from the Sandy Row area of Belfast and re-erected in the museum.

43 Dublin city, South Circular Road, Dolphin's Barn – red-brick terraced housing with projecting bay windows and patterned brickwork details. Still in a classical vein, but less refined than the earlier eighteenth-century houses.

43

44 Kircubbin, Co. Down, Main Street – Typical early nineteenth-century street with shops, houses and church. The church, though architecturally different from the rest of the street, maintains the essential rhythm. Its narrow front helps in this respect. Unfortunately, the buildings on the other side of the church make little contribution to the quality of the street.

45 Cashel, Co. Tipperary, Main Street – Some towns still possess fine groups of shops, which, because of their high individual qualities and their relationship to one another, are an important part of the local architectural heritage. They should be on the local preservation list but their best hope of protection is when their owners appreciate and are proud of their intrinsic qualities.

In the cities and some larger towns towards the end of the century new streets and squares were laid out, mostly in brick and in a variety of designs. The lower basement floor became less common, and external steps were used to emphasise the distinction between the main entrance and the lower floors. Brick became quite fashionable and is a distinguishing mark of many of the more substantial houses built in this period. Initially the smaller houses were utilitarian in appearance and had few of the picturesque details which were fashionable later. The larger houses, however, were more elaborate. Bay windows became more common together with the use of brick mouldings, string courses and cornices and elaborately carved door mouldings. Stone was sometimes used to highlight certain features. Generally the houses were more solid-looking than the earlier classical examples. The slim and elegant glazing bars of the Georgian period were now out of fashion.

In the north-east of Ulster, the industrial revolution influenced the rate and also the type of housing development. As we have seen, many Ulster towns expanded considerably during this period. Houses were provided on a vast scale for the workers, nearly all two-storey but with occasional rows of cottages. They were small, of the two-down-two-up type, with a tiny yard at the rear. The Ulster Folk Museum has re-erected streets of small houses from the Sandy Row area of Belfast. These houses may actually pre-date the mainstream of the industrial period, but they were the forerunners of the traditional workers' houses. They are described in the Museum information sheets as follows:

These houses are older than the others in the Sandy Row area, and indeed older than most others surviving in Belfast. They have some interesting features. For instance, the only way to get in and out of the back yard is through the houses; and the rooms are less than 8 ft. high inside. Both of these features were prohibited by Belfast housing bye-laws in 1845 and 1878, so that houses built after 1845 had to have larger rooms, and after 1878 a 'back entry'. Each house had two bedrooms upstairs, with another two rooms downstairs more recently known as the 'parlour' or 'kitchen parlour' and 'scullery' or 'working kitchen'.

As re-built at the folk museum, the houses are furnished as they would have been found about 1900 to 1910. While the whitewashed

exterior had survived up to their removal, only one original window frame and a few shutter hinges remained to suggest the older external appearance of the terrace. During the 1900-1910 period the larger front room was still being used as the kitchen with an open cooking hearth. Between 1905 and 1912 Belfast Corporation provided free gas fittings to working-class houses, including a gas meter, a single light-and-tap bracket, a gas ring and a flexible hose for the ring. This gas ring sat on the hob by the fire, and was used for quicker cooking. It was not until after the 1920s that gas cookers were issued, and then the back room, which had been a bedroom or a second room for preparing food, became the 'working kitchen' and the front room came to be known as the 'kitchen parlour'. Mains water was introduced to Rowland Street in the 1880s, and at this time the tap was often in the front kitchen, but in later years it was moved either out into the back yard, or (with the gas cooker) into the back room when it became the 'working kitchen'.

Ulster experienced the industrial revolution later than mainland Britain and as a result there were few of the back-to-back houses which were a feature of some English industrial cities. The street layout was rigid and utilitarian. There was an absence of features such as crescents and squares. Initially they had few of the picturesque details, for example porches and gables, which became quite fashionable later. The mills and workshops were closely integrated with the houses. They dominated the lives of the residents, not only socially and economically, but physically. Brick was universally used in a plain and severe manner. There was little ornamentation, except occasionally coloured brick around the window and odd panels of terracotta. Over the years, however, many occupants asserted their own personalities by painting or re-pointing with coloured mortars, and in some cases by white-washing. This was not always in the best of taste, but it created a sense of vitality and concern.

A feature of this period were the charitable trusts and commercial and industrial companies, who became involved in interesting and attractive housing developments. The Dublin Artisan Dwelling Company, established in 1876, was responsible for an extensive range of housing throughout Dublin, mostly small houses as the name of the company suggests. Their efforts made a great

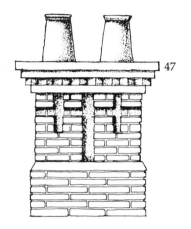

46 Trim, Co. Meath, Castle Street – a group of houses dating from the early 1900s, erected by the local council. They have a clearly defined architectural expression.

47 Dublin city, Estate Avenue (off Merrion Road) – Pembroke Estate houses. This charming group of houses is similar to many erected by the Pembroke Estate Company during the late nineteenth century. They were built by the company for its workers. A combination of brick and stone details with interesting roof-line and porches, they are typical of the cosy charm associated with this type of housing. They were sturdily built, have lasted well and are now much sought after.

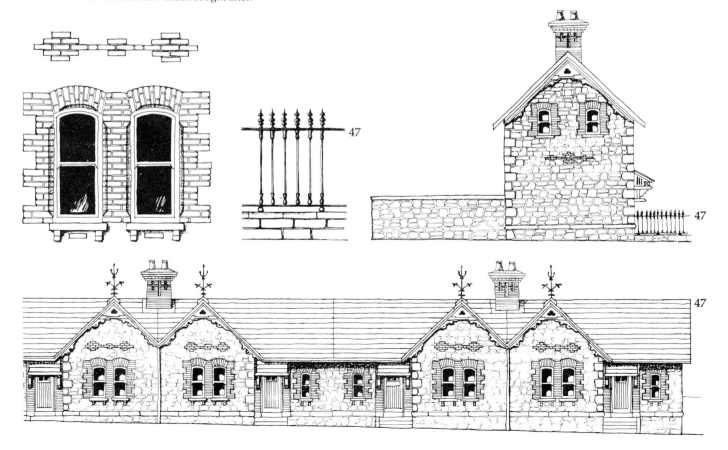

43

48

48 Loughrea, Co. Galway, Barrack Street – This house, dating from the 1930s, is in a mixture of styles, classical and Tudor.

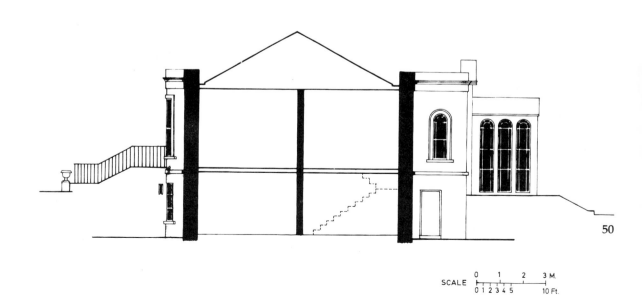

50

SCALE

0   1   2   3 M.

0 1 2 3 4 5   10 Ft.

49

49 Bandon, Co. Cork, North Main Street – large three-storey town houses built on narrow plots, dating probably from the mid-nineteenth century, but still influenced by classical styles. The bright colours are typical of many West Cork towns.

50 Seapoint, Co. Dublin, Brighton Vale – typical seaside villas in an Italianate style with fine plasterwork. The sunken lower floor effectively reduces the scale of the buildings and such houses often look much smaller than they actually are. The low 'villa type' appearance was considered appropriate for maritime situations, though similar houses were also built in other suburban localities. Simple exteriors often mask interiors of great quality and charm. A section appears opposite, on page 44.

50

contribution to the housing programme of the time. The street layout was typically formal and severe, and the houses were pleasantly designed in a faintly classical manner rather than a picturesque Gothic style. They were less severe than the traditional industrial housing and were well constructed, mostly in brick with slate roofs. The plots were quite small and there was a mixture of single- and two-storey housing. The greatest concentration is to be found in the small streets off the South Circular Road. Today these houses are still in good condition and have changed less than other houses of the period. They are now much sought after, and the humble artisan dwelling of a century ago is often the sophisticated 'town pad' of young executives, or the bijou home of the modern couple.

Small groups of houses were also built, often on a charitable basis, by a landlord, but more often by an industrial, commercial or special trust, such as the Pembroke Estate and Iveagh Trust in Dublin, and the railway companies in many towns throughout the country. A feature of some groups is their enthusiastic embracing of a friendly Gothic style, with high-pitched roofs, projecting gables, picturesque doorways, small-paned windows and other such details. These houses are full of charm and vitality. They are of social interest and in their distinctive way have added to the architectural heritage of the country.

Architectural fashions in housing do not change abruptly, particularly not in smaller towns. There are often examples in smaller towns of houses which retain the general simplicity and characteristics of the classical period. In this sense they ignore all the contemporary trends and have retained a style more common a hundred years earlier. The traditional building type in the smaller town, a two-storey house with two or three bays, plaster finish and no frills, was still cheaper to build than a brick house. In the later nineteenth century plaster-work was more ornate and adventurous, reflecting the general architectural standards of the period. In many provincial towns elaborate and flamboyant plaster facades were applied to existing shops and houses where the craftsman introduced a host of details incorporating traditional and classical motifs. The plasterer was an important tradesman of this period, much in demand, and in some parts of the country has left an interesting and distinctive legacy of craftsmanship, as did Pat McAuliffe in North Kerry and West Limerick.

There was little re-development or renewal and most housing was erected on new land and in the outskirts of existing towns. The traditional building unit was still the terrace, although later the detached and semi-detached house became more popular. Improvements in transportation influenced the location of new houses: many existing settlements within reach of the city centres, if served by the railway, became popular as residential suburbs, particularly for the more prosperous merchant and professional classes.

Large houses were built in a variety of styles with many variations on the Gothic and Tudor styles, using brick, stone, half-timbered gables, elaborate moulding and carvings and other details. Sometimes the overall effect was gracious and harmonious; sometimes unusual and eccentric or even dramatic and showy. Highly romantic mock medieval castles and Italianate villas with towers, campaniles and turrets were built. The grounds were spacious and luxurious, often of five acres or more, with attractive gate-lodges and perhaps smaller cottages for the staff. In 1880 *The Irish Builder*, an architectural magazine, sponsored a competition for gate-lodges, which shows the popularity of such developments.

Not all suburban houses were spacious and luxurious. Many smaller houses were built which were generally less ornate but nevertheless more elaborate than similar houses in town centres. Most of these late nineteenth-century houses still remain today, quite a number as dwelling houses. Others have been converted into hotels and guesthouses and some have been acquired by building firms, who demolished them and laid the grounds out as modern housing estates.

The railways gave a dramatic impetus to seaside holidays. A new type of house became a feature of these resorts. They were usually built in long terraces, three to four storeys high, finished in plaster and painted in bright colours. Architecturally there was a mixture of styles. Some terraces were restrained, in the classical vein, but were enlivened by ornamental plasterwork. In other cases the houses showed strong influences of the Gothic style with high roofs,

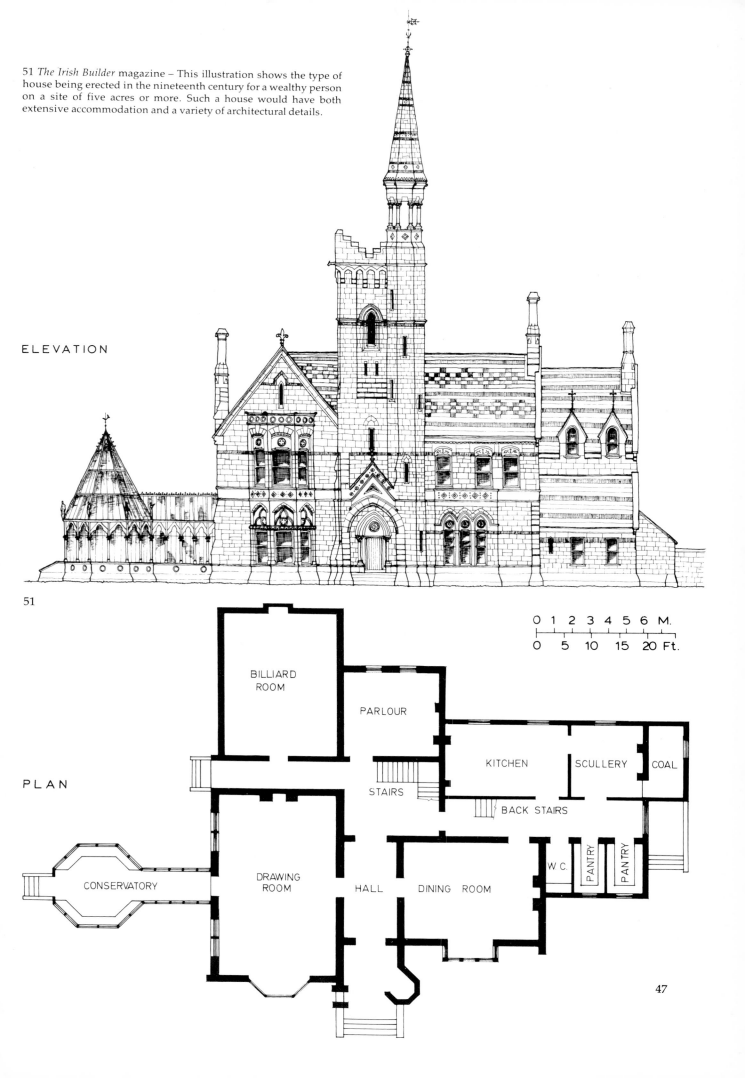

51 *The Irish Builder* magazine – This illustration shows the type of house being erected in the nineteenth century for a wealthy person on a site of five acres or more. Such a house would have both extensive accommodation and a variety of architectural details.

ELEVATION

51

PLAN

BILLIARD ROOM

PARLOUR

KITCHEN

SCULLERY

COAL

STAIRS

BACK STAIRS

CONSERVATORY

DRAWING ROOM

HALL

DINING ROOM

W.C.

PANTRY

PANTRY

0 1 2 3 4 5 6 M.

0 5 10 15 20 Ft.

52

52 Ballymena, Co. Antrim, Clonavon Street – These nineteenth-century mill workers' houses are built of local basalt stone with brick surrounds to the windows. The accommodation is limited – two rooms downstairs, two rooms upstairs – but the houses are sturdy and of a higher standard than most houses of the period. They have recently been restored by the Northern Ireland Housing Executive and provided with modern amenities.

GROUND FLOOR   FIRST FLOOR   ATTIC   52

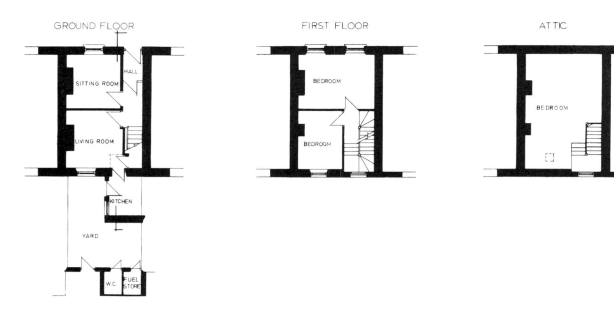

53 Ballymena, Co. Antrim, Grace Hill Road – a flamboyant mixture of architectural details, typical of the large detached house built around the turn of the century.

54 Limerick city, Ballinacurra – early twentieth-century houses in a flamboyant mixture of Tudor with arts and crafts style. They are narrow fronted and though the accommodation might not be much different from the earlier, more simple, Georgian style the outward expression is much more elaborate.

53

54

bay windows, projecting gables and ornate balustradings.

There were many other delightful seaside houses, single- and two-storey villas, small terraces, and occasionally grander houses in opulent gardens benefiting from maritime climate. The architectural styles were broadly similar, but there were many subtle variations in plan. The commonest theme was, of course, the highly ornamental use of plasterwork and bright colours. These houses were built in a so-called maritime architectural style, common throughout these islands but invariably influenced by local characteristics. The larger houses of the period were extremely ornate internally, with much use of plaster mouldings, colourful stained glass and high quality joinery in pine or mahogany. It was architecture of an expressive and confident type. The methods of construction and craftsmanship were more robust than in the earlier Georgian period, and these buildings are generally as structurally sound today as when they were first built. There was obviously widespread availability of first-class materials – stone wherever necessary, good quality brick, high-class and well-conditioned timber and a variety of roofing materials.

Following the Local Government Act of 1898 the newly established urban district councils and county councils were now responsible for public housing in their areas. This gave an added impetus to an already developing movement which was later to grow even more. The public housing of this period usually retained the traditional terrace form – two-storey and single-storey – and incorporated many of the pleasant architectural details common in other housing of the period. The new councils also built individual cottage-type housing similar to cottages in the countryside. An architectural competition was held at the turn of the century by the local authorities to stimulate ideas for the design of urban cottages. As a result of this competition many attractive houses were built in various parts of the country, based on ideas submitted in the competition. It was considered important that in addition to being functional and durable, the new public housing should look as attractive as possible. The Gaelic revival of this time influenced cultural matters, particularly in literary and, to a lesser extent, artistic work. However, its influence on architecture was slight and limited mainly to church building, although some plaster-work did incorporate motifs based on Celtic designs. In essence, therefore, this was a time of greater variety in domestic architecture. While space standards varied, style was important and the quality of building skills was uniformly high.

1920 - 1950

From the 1920s onwards a number of developments influenced the type and style of housing. The most fundamental was the increasing use of the motor car, which was quickly breaking down the distinction between town and country. Another important factor was that the detached or semi-detached house was now considered the most appropriate form of housing for the middle class, which was growing in extent and power. As a result, this period witnessed the beginnings of the modern housing estate consisting mainly of detached and semi-detached houses built at some distance from existing centres. More often than not the new houses were located on the main approach roads beginning the trend of ribbon development still common today. Initially architectural styles were varied, carrying on Victorian traditions, but the picturesque arts and crafts style was also popular.

The arts and crafts movement, which flourished in the early part of the century, was founded primarily as a reaction against the uniformity and mechanisation of the industrial revolution. It sought to popularise the traditions and values of hand-made artifacts, including furniture, tapestries and many other items in everyday use. The parallel Art Nouveau movement found its artistic inspiration in the complexities and intricacies of natural forms. In domestic architecture it was the age of the 'picturesque' – a style popular in Britain which in the early part of the century achieved extremely high standards indeed. It is understandable that its influence spread to Ireland in time. Houses with rather dramatic roofs, recessed doorways, half-timbered elevations and latticed windows became popular. There was an attempt to recreate a romanticism associated with small medieval houses of which there were very few in Ireland at the time.

The pace of housing development, however, was not great. In most towns the number of new houses could be counted individually and it is only in the larger centres that there is any significant number, mainly in the form of housing estates. The

ELEVATION

SCALE
0   1   2   3M
0   5   10Ft.

55

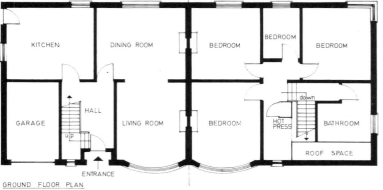

KITCHEN   DINING ROOM   BEDROOM   BEDROOM   BEDROOM

GARAGE   HALL   LIVING ROOM   BEDROOM   HOT PRESS   BATHROOM

up

down

ROOF SPACE

ENTRANCE

GROUND FLOOR PLAN

55 Dublin city, Mount Merrion – inter-war speculative houses. These houses are laid out in the 'Garden City' manner – good landscaping, spacious sites. This architectural style, with its long roofs, attractive porches and informal appearance, is again becoming popular.

56

56 Callan, Co. Kilkenny, Congress Road – local authority housing from the late 1930s, typical of houses built by county councils. They are small, three-bedroomed houses in an architectural style that is again becoming popular. The long sloping roofs were much used at this time. Walls were likely to be of mass concrete, windows were of steel and roofs were tiled.

57 Castlerea, Co. Roscommon, Ballintobber Road – a pair of semi-detached houses c. 1940s, in a picturesque style.

57

layout of the new estates from the thirties onwards was influenced by the Garden City movement. This movement was established in Britain by Ebenezer Howard and others and its primary aim was to develop a new concept of urban living, one which would seek the best advantages of both town and countryside. These 'new towns', as they were called, would have all the facilities of the town – schools, libraries, recreation halls, playing fields – but they would also have fresh air, space, landscaping and the natural forms of the countryside. It was essentially a continuation of previous attempts at reforming housing design and layout and social attitudes initially made by people like Robert Owen at New Lanark in Scotland as a reaction against the tightly packed towns of the industrial revolution. Architecturally the houses were in the picturesque tradition. They exhibit a charm and quality of design not often found in similar housing types of today. In estates such as Mount Merrion in Dublin there is also a refreshing variety of house types allied to an informality of layout. These houses, both individually and as groups, are now increasingly recognised as distinctive elements in the heritage of domestic architecture.

There was also a significant change in the use of building materials – concrete blocks with plastered finish, tiled roofs instead of slates, and the timber window giving way to steel. The new materials did not, however, affect overall quality, particularly when handled by a designer skilled in the art of housing design. Individual houses varied from the relatively simple to the grand type. There was less emphasis on the Gothic and the extravagances of the high Victorian period. Houses were smaller but exhibited great subtlety, both in external elevation and interior layout. Sites were still relatively large, but internal planning became less complicated. In some ways it was a return to Georgian simplicity, or perhaps it heralded the sparseness of the modern house plan.

Public housing became more widespread, and in some areas constituted the bulk of new developments. It still retained a terrace form, particularly in the larger centres. The architectural designs were still gently picturesque, but with less expressive details than previously. In smaller towns the public housing was usually a mixture of semi-detached cottages and houses. Sites were extensive, influenced by the rural tradition, and provided enough land to allow cultiv-

ation of basic foods, in strong contrast to the public housing provided today in these towns. High standards of craftsmanship were achieved. Expensive materials, by today's standards, were often used. It was not uncommon to use stone in those areas where it was traditional. Roofs were generally of slate, although later tiles were more common. In the large urban areas plot sizes were quite small, often with small yards rather than gardens, so there was an interesting contrast between quite high-density housing in the cities and extremely low-density in the smaller towns, which is not the case today as housing becomes even more standardised.

Another interesting development in domestic architecture, although to a lesser extent than in other European countries, was the modern movement. Here and there throughout the country there are examples of houses built in the new style, the forerunners of what was to come in later years – flat roofs, absence of ornamentation, an austere approach to details and horizontal rather than vertical emphases to windows. These early modern houses, although few in number, make a distinctive contribution to the evolution of the Irish house: they are now an important part of the architectural heritage. However, the modern style had a greater influence in the commercial and institutional fields than in domestic architecture. Fundamentally the developments of the modern movement are stylistic rather than practical, much as the romantic and earlier Gothic styles had been. Internally there was no great revolution in house planning or arrangement of rooms. Domestic life has, in architectural terms, changed less than many other things throughout history. The change from a servant–orientated household to a family- and machine-orientated one has been dramatic, but it influenced the size rather than the design of houses. The basic functions of eating, sleeping, and working remain the same, and in most people's opinion they are best carried out in separate rooms. The idea of the open-plan house has not become popular, and a traditional concern for privacy, both internal and external, is probably part of the reason for this. Domestic architecture concerns the evolution and development of styles, good design and layout and high quality craftsmanship rather than basic changes in the philosophy of living. Whether architectural expression is modern or in a supposedly old-fashioned

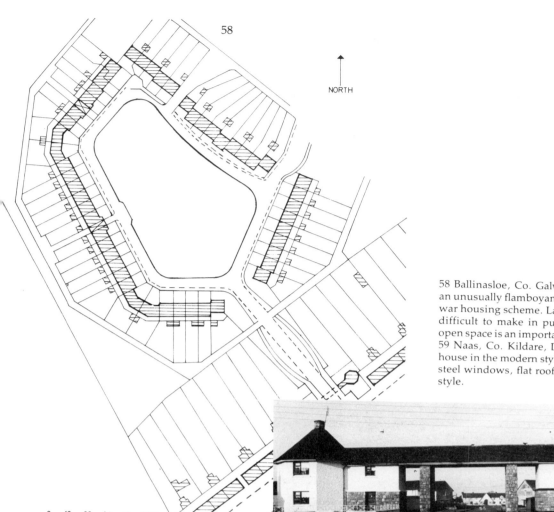

58

58 Ballinasloe, Co. Galway, Brackernagh Street –
an unusually flamboyant entrance to an early post-
war housing scheme. Later, such gestures became
difficult to make in public housing. The central
open space is an important element in the scheme.
59 Naas, Co. Kildare, Dublin Road – a detached
house in the modern style: clean lines, white walls,
steel windows, flat roofs. A good example of this
style.

NORTH

SCALE

| 0 | 10 | 20 | 30 | 40 | 50 M. |
| 0 | 50 | 100 | 150 Ft. |

59

style is less important than its quality and the way in which it is carried out.

POST-WAR HOUSING

The late forties and fifties was a period of major development, particularly in public housing. Many schemes were built throughout the country in the flush of post-war reconstruction. The terrace was universal and was used even in the smaller settlements. Occasionally design continued on pre-war patterns and the influence of the Garden City style is clear. Perhaps this was because old plans were revived after the war. The influence of modern architectural ideas and building methods became more obvious: the casement window replaced the up-and-down sash window, finishes were mainly in cement plaster, slate as a roofing material became a rarity and was superseded by tiles, elevations became more bland, and porches and gable fronts were no longer built. The houses were predominantly two-storey with the occasional single-storey group. Plot sizes became standardised in both town and country. In public housing schemes there was little provision for the motor car, which was understandable at the time, but in later years this was to cause many problems. Internal planning was relatively rigid – three-bedroomed houses being the norm – but the universal provision of internal bathroom and toilet facilities was an improvement over pre-war schemes. However, the overall impact was less satisfactory because of the extensiveness of many schemes. There was also a tendency to combine housing layout with future road building, which in the long run has proved unsatisfactory. The most successful housing schemes of this period are undoubtedly the smaller ones, where there was still an emphasis on informality. When landscaped and well maintained these can look quite attractive.

Private housing estates were still generally confined to the larger settlements. Housing immediately after the war continued in the picturesque tradition of the thirties and as with public housing, older house plans were still being used. Individually-built houses – detached or semi-detached – were built on the outskirts of towns. As a general rule house sizes were decreasing, but house plots were still relatively large. Comparatively few houses were built in a completely modern style, and the influence of the modern movement was more obvious in details than in the overall conception – large windows, flat-roofed garages, less variation in external appearance and more simplified internal planning. The standard of construction remained quite high. Individual houses were generally architect-designed and estates were developed by builders using their own technical resources. The 'lumping system', in which significant portions of the work are subcontracted out and which has brought a catastrophic decline in building standards in today's housing market, had not yet appeared. But generally the pace of housing development was slow and leisurely compared with the explosion which was to take place in the sixties and seventies.

Since the sixties there have been tremendous changes in the entire field of housing. The pattern book for individual houses became popular after a lapse of many years but the new standard plans were rarely based on sound architectural traditions. They paid little attention to site planning, orientation and landscaping. There is little consistency in architectural ideas, and ignorance is widespread. Architects became less involved in house design, particularly in the private sector. In the cities and in many medium-sized towns the private housing estate became the commonest form of housing. These estates range from small groups of houses to large amorphous developments with a thousand or more houses and a bigger population than most towns. These huge estates were built rapidly: the developers' sole concern and responsibility was with houses. The provision of schools, parks, shops and other community facilities lagged behind. Houses and plot sizes continued to decrease in size. Densities in some private estates equalled those in the public sector. The private market embraced a wide spectrum from basic three-bedroomed, semi-detached houses with few extras which were little different from public housing to expensive detached houses. Layouts became sterile and stereotyped. Planning regulations, particularly in such matters as road widths and types of road junctions, were given more consideration than individual design and landscaping. The tradition of creating a sense of place, through the disposition of the buildings and public spaces was largely ignored. In a period of rapid population growth, however, this is only to be expected. The emphasis shifted from the public to the private sector with an unfortunate consequent loss of architectural quality.

It is difficult in the early eighties to evaluate fully the different aspects of architectural development evident in the current housing phase. It is hard not to accept the conclusion that quality has been lost in the pursuit of quantity and profit. Standards have also declined in public housing more as a result of rigid layouts than of change in the design of individual houses.

Within the last few years there has been another radical shift in house design. A mock Georgian style is now rampant in cities and small towns, embracing both small cottage-style houses and large and extravagant dwellings, with small-paned windows, classical details in plastic or fibreglass and brick or plaster finishes. This is perhaps a result of the general public reaction against modern architecture and growing nostalgia for previous styles. It has dangerous implications, however. There is little awareness that individual housing design, and perhaps more importantly housing layout, is a task requiring design skills, sensitivity to the landscape and a wide knowledge of architectural styles. Such talents are not universal, even among trained architects.

Historical guide to House Types

A simplified guide to common house types in towns. There are of course many derivatives and there is no distinct break between the periods – Georgian-type houses were built in the late nineteenth century and modern-style houses in the 1930s.

1

1700–1850

1 Classic Georgian house: central hall; two-storey over basement; could be detached, semi-detached or terraced with archway to rear.
2 Large town house: usually built in terraces and in brick or stone, depending on locality.
3 Smaller town house, again in terraces.
4 Cottage: possibly a rebuilding on early medieval foundations; may originally have been thatched; now usually slated or occasionally with iron roof; some may be quite old.
5 Street house in smaller town: usually built of local stone with plastered walls; they have long gardens.
6 Street house: more common in cities; one-storey over basement; often in brick.

2

3

5

6

4

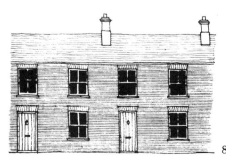

7

8

1850-1920

7 Brick-fronted two storey house, often with bay windows and patterned brickwork.

8 Two-storey house: plainer and smaller than 7; typical of industrial and artisan houses; common in Ulster.

9 Single-storey version of 8: brick-fronted; plot size usually quite small; 7, 8, 9 found mostly in cities and large towns.

10 Large house, late nineteenth-century: influenced by Gothic and other styles; built of local stone and often plastered with elaborate details; bay windows; commonly found in resort towns.

11 Tudor revival: timber framing and plaster panels; projecting first floor; usually two-storey; more commonly found in cities.

12 Romantic Gothic style: popular with estates, charitable and commercial organisations; high roofs, projecting porches, leaded windows.

1920-1950

13 Picturesque arts and crafts styles: popular with speculative builders; concrete walls, plastered, tiled roofs; detached and semi-detached.

14 Another variation of 13: essentially a dormer bungalow, built on the then outskirts of towns.

15 Forerunner of the modern bungalow: double fronted bay window; concrete walls, plastered; tiled or slated roof.

16 Early public housing: influenced by Gothic and arts and crafts styles; concrete walls, slated roofs; built in terraces; often with substantial back gardens.

1950 to 1960s

17 Public housing: built in terraces; plastered walls, steel windows, tiled roofs; window sizes becoming larger.

18 Private houses: usually semi-detached with attached garage; half brick front, large horizontal windows, plastered walls, tiled roof.

19 Modern style: dating from the 1930s; flat roof, white walls, steel windows, austere appearance; mostly detached and privately built.

20 Modern bungalow: a mixture of materials; large horizontal windows, tiled roof, attached garage; common all over the country; based on a traditional shape, has evolved into a multitude of designs; usually built on the outskirts of towns.

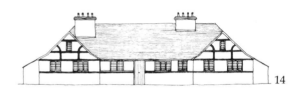

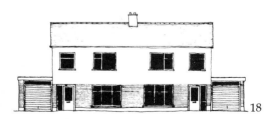

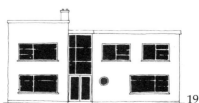

Chapter Five

Public and Community Buildings

Towns serve as social, administrative and religious centres, for their inhabitants and for people in the surrounding countryside. This social and administrative function is reflected in the nature and type of public buildings in towns. The smallest villages would usually have a church and school, some indeed more than one church. Any town that prided itself on its status would also have a market house and perhaps a court-house. These buildings represented the traditional role of the establishment, the church in its religious buildings and schools, the landlord in the development of fairs and markets and the influence of law and administration in the court-house.

In the nineteenth century the State became increasingly involved in the day-to-day activities of people. The seeds of modern bureaucracy were being sown. This new involvement in community life resulted in the development of interesting building types, and in addition made a valuable contribution to the heritage of local architecture which is still evident today. The architectural styles chosen for the various buildings reflected accurately the prevailing trends of the day. The public buildings erected in the eighteenth and early nineteenth centuries are generally in the classical style, reflecting Georgian architectural ideas. From the mid-nineteenth century onwards public architecture generally assumed a variety of styles, notably the Gothic, but the Italianate and classical styles always remained popular. There were also individual styles based on the designer's personal interpretation of current fashion. The different types of public buildings are worthy of special study in themselves: here they are only treated in

general. Architecturally outstanding public buildings are generally widely recognised and cherished, but their lesser-known counterparts such as the ordinary church, school or hall are taken for granted, and their architectural qualities and significance are underestimated.

The larger towns and cities have a wide range of public buildings dating from every period. There are churches of many denominations and schools, which are usually, but not always, associated with the churches. The nineteenth-century Education Acts generated a great phase of school building. The Poor Law and Public Health Acts resulted in the building of the workhouses and the improvement of existing charitable institutions whose major objective was the health and well-being of ordinary people. The new local government bodies, which had taken over from the grand juries, were responsible for the building of town halls, libraries and other buildings as well as housing. The needs of public order and military policies influenced the building of police and military barracks. As the State's involvement increased, the public building types became more diverse.

Public institutions were fully aware of their social importance and so external appearances were significant. The buildings not only had to function well but had to have an architectural dignity commensurate with their particular social purpose. Since the 1940s the State has been involved in community life at all levels and public buildings have been increasing in number, size and complexity. The requirements of today however, are quite different, not least in relation to traffic and technological developments. There is less variety in architectural styles and the modern style is almost universally used. However, to be really successful this style demands a high level of skill, commitment and understanding, which are unfortunately rare. Public reaction against modern architecture in recent years has affected the design of public buildings. New approaches are being considered which, while not necessarily copying historic styles, acknowledge in certain ways the standards and traditions they have established.

CHURCHES

Religious activity in towns was organised in parish units. In rural areas, the focus of activity, the parish church, might be located in a town, but the parish itself could embrace the surrounding countryside. In the smaller towns, and to a surprising extent in the cities, social life was largely influenced by church activities. Most towns, even quite small ones, had Roman Catholic and Church of Ireland churches and many would also have churches of other denominations – Methodist, Presbyterian, and the smaller Christian religions. The small town of Ramelton in County Donegal has no less than seven churches, all architecturally interesting. To the ordinary people the church was the most important public building in their community. Its building and upkeep usually commanded the maximum resources, both architecturally and financially. Despite their widespread distribution, and a general uniformity of activities, there was little standardisation in church architecture, although in certain districts some churches do have a broadly similar appearance. This may be due to the influence of an architect working in a particular area.

However, over the years the various religious denominations favoured certain styles, which can be easily recognised. For example, many Catholic churches date from the latter part of the nineteenth century, and a forceful Gothic style was popular with their priests and architects. These churches often replaced earlier ones, and some parishioners must have felt concern and regret at the loss of old and familiar structures, though there are few recorded instances of such concern being expressed openly. It was not yet the era of public participation. The Church of Ireland churches, the great majority of which are pre-1850, were mostly classical in style, or had a certain Gothic quality, for example in the use of pointed arches in windows and doors or a battlemented square tower, with or without a spire. The Methodists and Presbyterians rarely used a formal Gothic style. Towers or spires were rare, but the pointed arch was more common. Their churches were essentially viewed as meeting halls with considerable lay involvement in the liturgical functions. Classical features, such as round-headed windows, porticos and columns, were common on Methodist churches. These are all general observations and there are exceptions to be found throughout the country, for instance classically inspired Catholic churches and Presbyterian churches in a relatively high Gothic style. Frequently the main determining factors were the period in which the church itself was built and the tastes and background of the individuals involved rather than its denomination.

The location of the church and its relationship to adjacent buildings add variety to the town. Quite often churches are set apart from other buildings and may form the dominant part of a religious complex within the town, including the church house, school, hall, graveyard and other elements. These groupings may share a common style or use a variety of styles, but, when graced with attractive and mature planting as they often are, they provide a most interesting contrast to the more formal arrangement of adjacent streets and squares and they create a distinctive sense of place. In other cases churches are fitted into the street pattern, where their different scale and sometimes monumental character make an interesting, if not always successful, foil to adjacent buildings.

In many towns, the Church of Ireland church commands a location of importance. It usually occupies a site of historical significance, around which the town may have developed. Occasionally the ruins of older churches are still evident, sometimes separated from the main building, which usually dates from the eighteenth or early nineteenth century. In other cases ruins are incorporated into the newer building. The towers of these churches and, if they have them, their elegant spires, are among the most attractive features of many towns. They were invariably built with local stone in a restrained and dignified manner. The sites often incorporate a small graveyard.

By the mid-eighteenth century the Penal Laws had been somewhat relaxed and Catholics were once again building churches. These early churches were small, generally

60 Callan, Co. Kilkenny, Green Street – Catholic church interior. This fine classical interior is still largely intact. (See page 68 for drawing of exterior.)

61 Antrim town, Church Street – First Presbyterian church. An impressive building in the Greek revival style with unusual and imposing portico.

62 Cootehill, Co. Cavan, Main Street – Church of Ireland church. This church, situated at the end of the main street, is a good example of a typical 'First Fruits' church. It is built of local stone with a west tower and simple Gothic lines.

63 Clonakilty, Co. Cork, Chapel Street – Catholic church. A fine example of the Gothic revival style, so popular with church authorities. An architectural demonstration of a resurgent church. The interior is particularly impressive.

barn-like or T-plan structures. They were built of stone with lime-plastered walls. Many had thatched roofs, though in larger towns slated roofs would have been more common. The interiors could be rather austere with whitewashed walls and flagged floors reflecting poor economic circumstances, but in some instances walls and ceiling were panelled giving a warm and intimate feeling more like a meeting room or substantial parlour than a traditional ecclesiastical interior. They were not high buildings and the average height from floor to eaves would have been not more than sixteen feet. In the T-plan churches galleries were often erected to maximise the use of space and to provide for growing congregations. These early churches are the beginnings of Catholic ecclesiastical architecture after the Reformation. They did not last long, particularly in the larger urban centres. In country areas and smaller villages they had a longer life and some still remain.

Later in the eighteenth and early nineteenth centuries, as the Catholic church became more confident and church members, particularly the merchant classes in the towns, became more prosperous, these early churches were replaced by more substantial and impressive buildings, particularly in the city centres and larger towns. They were generally built in the classical or Gothic styles. Widespread use of the full Gothic revival style was to come later in the nineteenth century, and its effects were more widespread, leaving an impressive legacy of churches in cities, small villages and the countryside.

Some architects, notably J. J. McCarthy, William Hague, J. J. O'Callaghan, were responsible for many churches in this high Gothic style, some cathedral-like in their scale and size. Built of granite and limestone, with extremely high standards in masonry, stone carving, joinery and marble work, they represent a high point in building craftsmanship unlikely to be repeated again for a long time, if ever.

The churches of other denominations are generally more restrained in architectural styles. The building reflects the size and prosperity of the particular community. For example, in the south, Methodist churches which would not be in every town, are generally small and self-effacing buildings, whereas, in some Ulster towns, they are large, not only in size but in architectural ideas. In Ireland the larger Methodist churches were designed like classical temples with impressive porticos and elaborately fitted interiors generally painted in bright colours. The churches of the smaller sects were domestic in character, with perhaps only a pointed or circular-headed window indicating a building of religious significance. The churches are an important part of the architectural heritage in any locality. They are invariably buildings of presence and interest, from the simplest chapel of a little-known group to the large and impressive nineteenth-century Catholic churches. Sometimes quite an ordinary exterior may conceal an interior of great interest and significance: the reverse is also often true.

Like other buildings, churches are now undergoing changes caused by social, economic and religious developments. Many city-centre churches are losing their congregations and are finding it difficult to maintain the fabric of the church. Some have been transformed to new uses; others are lying empty and falling into dilapidation. These changes affect churches of the Protestant denominations more than Catholic churches. In the Republic of Ireland most Protestant churches in the smaller settlements also have declining congregations. In some instances there are only a few family groups still attending, and the burden of maintenance is extremely high. Others are empty and occasionally in a ruinous condition. It is sad when the local Protestant church falls into disuse, as it usually occupies a prominent place in the physical and architectural structure of the town and its dilapidated appearance will detract from the town's overall qualities. The disused church becomes only a physical reminder of a congregation perhaps now but a memory only, but which in its day contributed much to the social and cultural heritage of its district. These churches are too important architecturally and socially to be allowed to decay. The stonework has mellowed gracefully over the years, and the overgrown graveyards have a variety of tombstones, ranging from extravagant mausoleums commemorating once powerful families of which all trace has now vanished to humble gravestones, and lonely trees standing guard, as it were, over departed congregations. A few churches have been converted to new uses but much remains to be done. The responsibility now falls on the local community. Converting old churches is a task which requires sensitivity and imagination, so that the new use enhan-

64 Dublin city, Fairview Road – Gospel Hall. This small building sits quietly but efficiently into the street surroundings and makes a valuable contribution to the unified street design.

65 Letterkenny, Co. Donegal, Sentry Hill Road – typical seminary built towards the end of the nineteenth century to cater for the education of priests and laity; an impressive building of stone in the Gothic style, but somewhat eccentric with a dash of 'Scottish baronial' style thrown in for good measure.

66 Roscrea, Co. Tipperary, Church Street – Church of Ireland church. An impressive building in the Gothic style. The interior has retained all its original characteristics. Slender columns and slightly vaulted ceiling create a space of lightness and elegance.

66

ces and respects the architectural dignity of the building and its social history.

The architectural character of many Catholic churches is also changing, not because of population decline, socio-economic trends, or religious indifference, but mainly because of new liturgical requirements and an increasing population. In the city centres the great shifts in population are affecting the viability of many public buildings and here the Catholic congregations also are declining, but the emphasis that Catholicism has traditionally laid on formal religious practice means that their churches are generally more intensely used. Approximately seventy-five per cent of the population of the whole of Ireland is Catholic, and a large proportion of these attend services regularly. The recent changes occasioned by current liturgical requirements unfortunately do not often respect the intrinsic architectural character of the church. An overwhelming desire for modernisation seems to afflict those responsible. The interiors of many churches were changed drastically. The high quality of craftsmanship, such a feature of the older churches, appears to have been largely unappreciated. Fine marble altars were insensitively modified and exquisite hand-made joinery unnecessarily replaced. Other items of furniture and fittings, specially designed and made as part of the original conception of the building, were replaced by mass-produced modern examples, which might be in sympathy with a modern church, but look wholly incongruous in a nineteenth-century building. External changes were equally unsympathetic: attractive tree-lined grounds were mutilated to provide more car-parking space.

The need for new Catholic churches continues. Each decade has witnessed the building of new churches, particularly in the city suburbs and expanding towns. Even where the population was relatively static, new churches were sometimes built to replace supposedly old-fashioned and structurally unsound buildings. The styles were varied. The 1920s witnessed the last of the stone-built churches in the Gothic manner. The classical style and the basilican plan, which never went completely out of fashion, became more common. Here and there are examples of modernised Hiberno-Romanesque and Byzantine styles. To build a high Gothic church in the mid-twentieth century would have been extremely expensive. The quality of workmanship was still good,

though not reaching the high standards of previous decades.

In recent years Catholic church building has continued. There has been a gradual move away from the old styles and the modern movement has had a significant influence on contemporary churches. In many ways modern churches are more suited to the new liturgy where community participation is important. The religious atmosphere in the traditional sense has now gone and the modern church is not always as immediately recognisable as its older counterpart.

In Northern Ireland Protestant churches have continued to be built, but not as much as Catholic churches. Architectural styles were equally varied with an emphasis on traditional forms until the post-war years when the transition towards modern styles was finally accomplished. It is too early yet to evaluate these modern churches architecturally. The relationship between the modern and the traditional is always difficult. Perhaps the most lasting modern churches will be those which utilised traditional styles in a sensitive and scholarly way despite the problems caused by modern materials and also those churches which are unashamedly modern, in a style that was carried through with skill and conviction and respect for the religious significance of the building.

SCHOOLS AND RELIGIOUS HOUSES

Religion and education have always been closely related, from the time of the medieval monasteries to the present day. The suppression of the monasteries in the sixteenth century meant the decline of educational establishments which had had a long and honoured history. The physical remains of these institutions are few: those that exist, are important historically, but do not quite fit our definition of local architecture, and they have been extensively written about.

Formal education in the modern sense began in the early part of the seventeenth century when it was decreed that the newly Planted areas would have free schools. These were the fore-runners of the royal schools later established by charter from Charles I, a number of which have continued in education until the present day. Other schools were later founded by interested landlords and private foundations, both religious and

67 Bailieborough, Co. Cavan, Church Street – model school, a sturdy building in the Gothic style. Good-quality stonework was a common feature of the model schools erected in various towns.

68 Dunmanway, Co. Cork, Ballineen Road – This vocational school dates from the 1950s. Many such buildings were erected around the country. They differed from the national schools in that they were usually designed by individual architects and were in the classical style popular from the twenties to the fifties for educational buildings.

69 Oldcastle, Co. Meath, Market Street – Gilson School. An impressive school in the classical style, designed by one of the most eminent architects of the day – C. R. Cockerell of London – who at that time was also carrying out other commissions for an important local family.

70 Dublin city, Richmond Street – Richmond Hospital. Built about the turn of the century, this is a flamboyant building in brick and terracotta, with many impressive details of cupolas, gables and so on – a 'free' Art Nouveau style. Visually, an extremely impressive building.

71 Mullingar, Castlepollard Road – This old workhouse is now part of a hospital. Externally, it retains many of its original characteristics.

72 Typical workhouse. This sketch illustrates, in diagrammatic form, the layout of a typical workhouse of the nineteenth century.

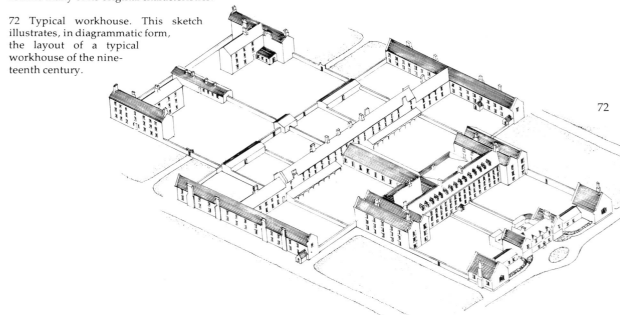

73

73 Ballycastle, Co. Antrim, The Diamond – The Church of Ireland church occupies an important position in the main square. It dates from the middle of the eighteenth century. Its elegant facade and interesting octagonal tower mark it out from the general run of small-town churches.

lay. Like other activities, these schools developed rapidly in the eighteenth and early nineteenth centuries and in general the buildings, which are not numerous but always interesting, date from this time. Education was a luxury available only to the wealthier classes and to the occasional gifted scholar with the patronage of the landlord. Even the so-called hedge schools whose activities probably took place in dwelling houses or even in outbuildings, were restrictive in their intake. Education began to influence local architectural styles from the mid-nineteenth century onwards, following the Education Act of 1831. This Act heralded the beginning of mass education, initially at primary level. A national system was established affording the opportunity to all who desired it to receive at least an elementary education. Schools only then became important and universally distinguished as a building type. In certain areas 'model schools' were established, which served as both teacher-training establishments and ordinary schools. They were interesting but not elegant buildings, substantially built with good quality stone walls and high slated roofs in a 'school Gothic' style broadly similar to other public buildings of the period. Examples are the model schools in Athy, Co. Kildare, and Bailieborough, Co. Cavan, which are still used largely for educational purposes.

Although the new national schools were State assisted, the churches were involved in their day-to-day running and the schools were organised on parish lines. A major programme of school building was commenced. Most towns had Catholic and Protestant schools. There were efforts to integrate the denominations but these failed. The earlier schools were frequently two-storey and occasionally incorporated a teacher's residence: Few early schools are still in use and most urban national schools today date from the late nineteenth century onwards. Later, as the new system developed, standard building types were widely used. The size varied from a three-roomed structure in a small town to quite large buildings in the single-storey rectangular building with three to five classrooms, and a limited range of ancillary facilities. These school buildings were domestic in scale and expression. Their appearance was rather severe, with little attempt at architectural frills, except when the manager, the parish priest or rector, had an interest in such matters. In larger communities, separate schools were provided for boys and girls, and in mixed schools separate entrances and playing areas for boys and girls were common.

Although rarely individually distinguished buildings, the simplicity of design and construction of these schools ensures that they fit successfully into the architectural character of towns, and they are an interesting aspect of local architectural heritage. Over the years their appearance has changed little. They are usually single-storey buildings with Georgian-style windows, slated roofs and lime plaster or, later, cement on the walls; in rare instances local stone was used. The internal arrangements and the basic classroom size have also remained the same, and a small national school built in the early sixties would be very similar to one erected at the turn of the century, except for the addition of modern facilities such as toilets and teachers' rooms. The more complex requirements of modern education, however, have resulted in a more diverse architectural style for present-day primary schools.

In the nineteenth century religious involvement in education at all levels, particularly by the Catholic church, increased. New religious orders were founded whose principal activities were in education and international orders became involved in this field. The Catholic religious orders were the powerhouse of education until recent changes diminished their influence.

New convents and other institutions were established on a widespread basis. Many towns have at least one building which provides a home for a religious order engaged either in education or other community activity. This religious and educational development has left a fine legacy of architecture distinctive in its appearance and style. Frequently built in a Gothic style, religious houses were generally substantial three- or four-storey buildings with high-pitched roofs, ornate chimneys, projecting gables and other Gothic details. They were built of good quality stone, coursed and pointed and often relieved by brick trim, or they were plastered and painted. Standards of craftsmanship in the stonework, brick detailing and roof treatments are extremely high. Internally there are fine individual rooms, particularly chapels and meeting rooms, with high quality woodwork and tiling.

It was common for those religious orders

74

75

PART ELEVATION

```
0        5         10M.
0    10      20    30Ft.
```

76

74 Omagh, Co. Tyrone, Asylum Road –
mental hospital. A building of high quality
with finely proportioned windows and
good stonework.

75 Sligo town, Dromahir Road – mental
hospital. This building is the centre of an
interesting complex. The large scale of such
buildings is impressive. Most were
individually designed and had their own
distinctive characteristics. Plans were
broadly similar – separate wings for male
and female patients and long corridors
serving treatment rooms and dormitories.

76 Ballinasloe, Co. Galway, Church Street –
mental hospital. A fine classical building
attributed to Francis Johnston, a famous
architect of the early nineteenth century.

77 Callan, Co. Kilkenny, Green Street – Catholic church in the classical style. The portico and spire were added later. The church is unusual in that it has living accommodation incorporated into the structure (see page 59 for photo of interior.)

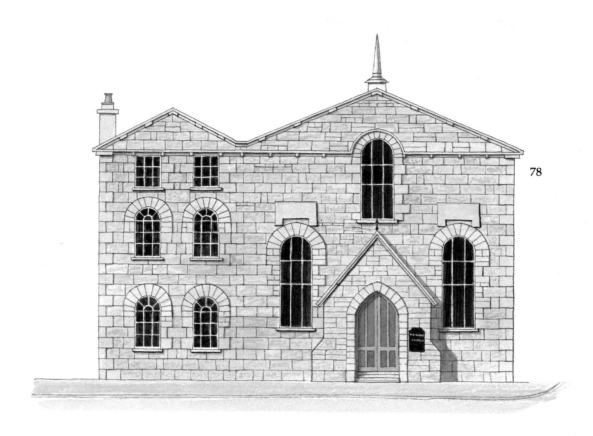

78

78 Galway city, Queen Street – The Methodist church with attached hall is a pleasantly proportioned building in a classical style forming an attractive feature at the end of the street.

79 Crumlin, Co. Antrim, Main Street – The Presbyterian church with ancillary buildings makes a pleasant contribution to the main street. Plastered walls and slated roof emphasise its simplicity.

79

established countrywide to use standard plans for their buildings, creating a sort of 'house style'. These large, rather austere buildings, with their dramatic roof lines can be quite striking. Occasionally a classical style was chosen, perhaps to fit in with the local architectural character or to suit the taste of the architect or the religious superior. They are an interesting building type, which has been relatively ignored to date. Occasionally they form part of the street pattern and here the classical style is more successful, but more frequently they are set apart from other buildings in well-wooded grounds, enclosed by high walls.

The establishment of the religious orders coincided with the decline of the large estate, and fortunately many fine houses, which otherwise might have fallen into disrepair, found caring new owners in the religious sisters and brothers. These religious buildings have generally retained their original character, particularly the convent interiors, where the sense of tidiness and order is unique. Like other nineteenth-century buildings, they are becoming more expensive to maintain. The decline in religious vocations has not helped matters and many are now under-occupied. Their future role as religious or educational buildings may be in doubt, but they must surely have potential for community uses, for example as residential apartments or craft centres.

Other denominations were also involved in education in the nineteenth century. New schools were established or older ones developed. Built in a variety of styles, they demonstrate the fine building techniques of the day, often serving both residential and educational needs.

Other educational developments which contributed to the quality of local architecture were the agricultural schools, which were established to foster new techniques in agriculture, and in the major urban areas technical institutes were established, which were the fore-runners of the vocational schools erected in many towns from the twenties and thirties onwards. Initially the architecture of these buildings was in the traditional mould of the period – single- or two-storey buildings with plastered concrete block walls, slated or tiled roofs and windows of classical proportions. Internally there was no great revolution in planning, most of the main teaching rooms opening off circulation corridors.

Feeding the poor and healing the sick has always been fundamental to community life. There is little physical evidence today of such activity in earlier times, except perhaps the alms houses previously mentioned. In the eighteenth century voluntary hospitals were established in the cities, a number of which are still in existence. Some, like the Rotunda Hospital in Dublin, are of great architectural significance, comparing favourably with any other public building of the period. These early hospitals were built in a classical style to the standard hospital plan of the period. The impetus for their establishment came from a variety of sources – physicians, socially concerned individuals and religious organisations.

From the nineteenth century onwards there was a great concern for the health and social well-being of the general public. As in other countries, the ordinary population lived in poor circumstances and the periodic famines, together with rapid population growth, added to the problems. The Poor Law Act of 1838 is of social and historical significance, but also had a considerable architectural impact throughout the country, perhaps more so than any single health-building programme before or since. The first task of the Poor Law Commissioners, established under the Act, was the provision of workhouses for the relief of the needy and destitute. To achieve this they set up their own technical and administrative offices. Few existing buildings were suitable for such uses and so it was decided to build new ones. The commissioners employed George Wilkinson as their architect. Wilkinson, an Englishman with experience of such work, took up duty in 1839. He set about inspecting sites, preparing plans, and supervising the work. He was obviously a person of tremendous energy and drive. By 1843, 112 workhouses were completed and seventeen others at an advanced stage.[1] The entire country was divided into Poor Law unions and each union had its workhouse, administered by a board of guardians. In 1847, 150 workhouses had been completed, 125 of which were entirely new buildings. This was a considerable feat, even for Victorian times, when the rate of achievement was extremely high, and unimaginable today. As might be expected, the workhouses were based on a standardised plan which varied only in relation to the amount of accommodation to be provided.

80 Cork city – Prince's Street markets. An enclosed shopping mall, the market fits neatly into the grid of small side streets in the city centre. Its front facade is an interesting essay in the Venetian style and it has a fine spacious interior with good quality cast-iron work as shown in the section and interesting roof lighting. The building has been superbly restored by Cork Corporation.

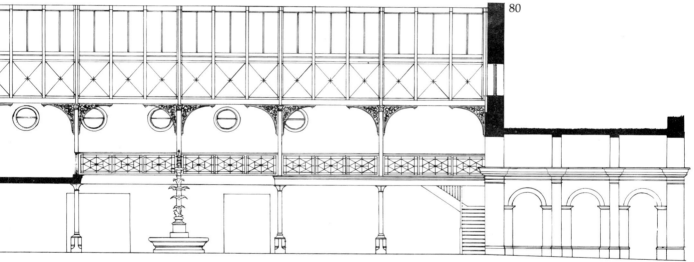

80

81 Dublin city, Francis Street – Iveagh markets. A combined market and public warehouse, the impressive architectural style of this building belies its rather humble uses.

81   71

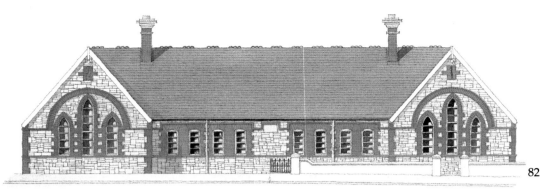

82

82 Kinnegad, Co. Westmeath, Main Street – This national school dates from the late nineteenth century. The use of brick and stone, together with the projecting gables, was typical of public buildings of that period. There is also a teacher's house at the rear in the same architectural style.

83

83 Moville, Co. Donegal, Greencastle Road – national school. A small school of simple expression, forerunner of many standard schools.

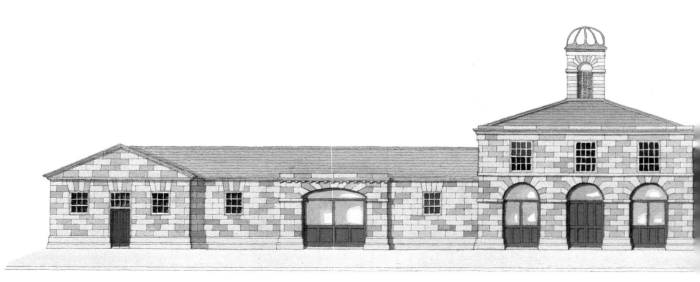

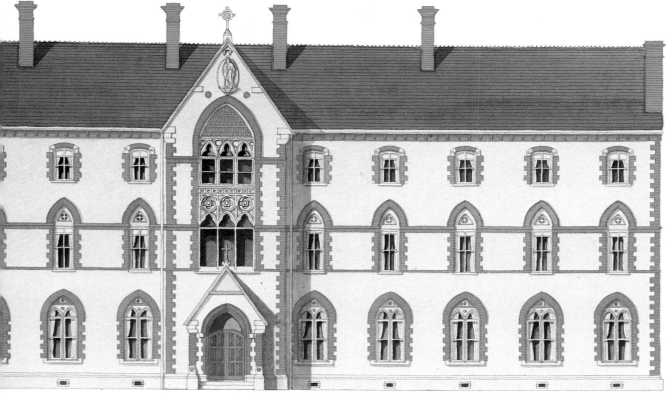

84

Kilcock, Co. Kildare, Church Street – Presentation
Convent. A typical late nineteenth-century ecclesiastical
building in the Gothic style with pointed windows and high
roof – a building of strength and quality. Internally it retains
its original characteristics, with superb joinery and
excellent tilework.

Drogheda, Co. Louth, Fair Street – the old corn exchange
and market, a finely executed classical building. Later extended to become a court-house and, later again, the town hall.
The fine classical features are still evident despite many
internal changes.

85

There was a small front block which acted as an admission area and accommodation for the warden. Behind that were the main buildings, usually of three or four storeys, with accommodation for men and women rigidly segregated. The central blocks were in the form of an H with communal facilities, chapel, dining halls and so on, forming the cross-bar of the H. Further behind were the infirmary, fever wards and accommodation for the sick. The disposition of the units created a series of yards which provided for outdoor recreation. The buildings were erected in stone, coursed and pointed. Inside, the walls were unplastered and whitewashed. Ground floors were usually of mortar or clay and the upper floor of timber. Roofs were slated and the general architectural style is in the Gothic manner.

Many workhouses remain throughout the country and a considerable number are used as hospitals of one sort or another which has meant significant changes in their appearance. Some have been demolished and others have been converted to different uses. Too often the alterations have been carried out with little sensitivity. Perhaps their architecture has never been fully appreciated. The very name of the workhouse is closely associated in many Irish minds with famine and misfortune. They were considered in the same way as jails, and perhaps they were like jails to many of their inmates. This negative attitude has distracted attention from their architectural and historical significance, but they are buildings of presence and style, and are an important social record of the period. The standard of craftsmanship, particularly the masonry work was extremely high, and today this particular quality is better appreciated. Where they still exist in their original form they are a significant part of the local architectural heritage.

The mental hospitals are another significant building venture from the mid-nineteenth century. Fewer than the workhouses, they were usually more substantial buildings. They had the same institutional appearance, as did many public buildings of the period. However, they were individually designed and were not part of a standardised building programme, although there are general similarities in layout. More money was available for their construction and dressed stone was used externally rather than coursed rubble. Brick was also used, particularly in those built towards the end of the century. The architectural styles are varied, ranging from the refined classical style in Ballinasloe, Co. Galway, and the slightly Gothic style in Sligo town, to the unusual Italianate style chosen for Enniscorthy, Co. Wexford, where the hospital was built in a dramatic location overlooking the River Slaney. Nearly all the mental hospitals are still in use and have developed into large institutions. They are traditionally self-contained establishments and include farms, workshops, churches and other buildings. Their grounds are extensive, well-wooded and usually immaculately maintained. Labour does not pose the same problems as in other public institutions. The quality and character of their surroundings contribute significantly to their appearance. Unfortunately there is rarely any architectural consistency about many recent additions, and it is the original buildings which remain of greatest interest and architectural character.

In the cities, hospital development continued in the nineteenth century, with the newly established religious and other charitable organisations in the vanguard. Their architectural character was equally diverse: classical, Gothic and a Dutch gable free style were all individually interpreted. The principal influence appears to have been the taste and approach of the architects involved.

In this century hospital building continued, but at a slower pace. More than most building types, hospitals are influenced by modern technology. Early twentieth-century architectural styles were traditional, in a classical vein, and achieved more flamboyant styles. The hospital at Portlaoise, Co. Laois, designed by Michael Scott, is an early and interesting example of the modern style, whereas the hospital at Tullamore, Co. Offaly also by Scott is more traditional in appearance, although the staircase windows are distinctly modern in conception. The modern style was not used to any great extent until the fifties, when building materials began to change, concrete and steel replacing stone and timber, and flat roofs taking over from the traditional pitched roof.

Other buildings that come under this classification include dispensaries. Each Poor Law union was divided into a number of dispensary districts under the charge of the local doctor. Such buildings are to be found throughout the country, sometimes purpose-built, sometimes adaptations of existing buildings. They are small in scale and domestic in character, and are often indistinguishable from houses.

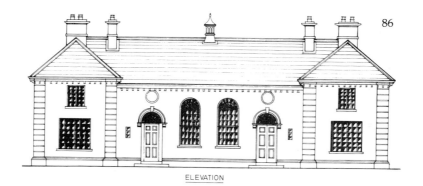

86

ELEVATION

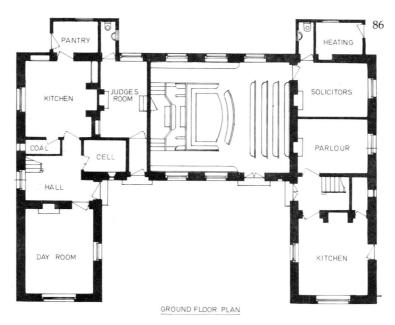

86

PANTRY

HEATING

KITCHEN

JUDGES ROOM

SOLICITORS

COAL

CELL

PARLOUR

HALL

DAY ROOM

KITCHEN

GROUND FLOOR PLAN

86 Dowra, Co. Cavan, Main Street – court-house and garda station. An unusually impressive public building surprising in a small rural village.

87 Mullingar, Co. Westmeath, Market Square – a market house commanding an important position and which has been improved in recent years.

87

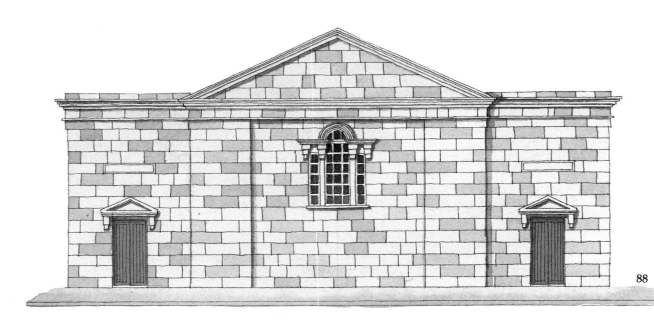

88 Bantry, Co. Cork, the Square – a small court-house with a rather severe appearance. It has only one court-room, with ancillary facilities. Similar court-houses were built in other southern towns, such as Kanturk, Millstreet, Midleton.

89 Ballycastle, Co. Antrim, Ann Street – True Blue Masonic Hall. A small hall in the classical style presented in an enthusiastic manner.

90 Nenagh, Co. Tipperary, Kickham Street – a substantial court-house of the type commonly built in large provincial towns. In the classical tradition, with impressive portico and commanding an important position. Internally, its plan provides two court-rooms, a central hallway and the usual offices.

91 Bangor, Co. Down, Hamilton Road – Orange Hall. Fitting neatly into a small-scale residential street, the hall, with its pointed windows and decorative mouldings, has an individual expression.

Today the emphasis on community health and social development is creating a new range of building types, for example health centres in place of the dispensaries, and geriatric homes locally based in place of the workhouse. Health buildings have rarely been considered architecturally significant as technological and social requirements obviously overshadowed other considerations, but many are architecturally interesting, despite conforming to the specific requirements of their day.

ADMINISTRATIVE BUILDINGS

Towns are centres of administration, and this fact is reflected in the range and type of buildings devoted to administrative purposes. Although there was a comprehensive range of boroughs in medieval times, which must have required some sort of administrative arrangements,there are few physical remains of such activities from the Middle Ages. Buildings in this category date from the eighteenth century onwards. The two aspects of administration that were considered important during the early phase of modern urban development were the legal system and the establishment and regulation of markets, so market houses and courthouses were among the first public buildings to be erected. They are usually buildings of distinction and importance in a prominent location and of high quality architecture.

Most towns have a market house which might be a small building fitting neatly between houses and shops. Large city markets may embrace different buildings and have enclosed spaces for selling and other activities. A local market always added to the commercial attractions of a town. The landlord, who in most instances was the driving force behind town improvements, was often personally responsible for the building of the market house, as many inscriptions testify. In smaller centres the buildings were straightforward and simple. An open area on the ground floor was used for trading and selling and the upper floor was perhaps used as a meeting hall. Market houses were strategically located and often formed the focal point in the principal space in the town where each week or each month the major economic activity of the district took place. Many market houses still remain and have retained their architectural quality to a large degree. The smaller market houses were well constructed. They were usually built of stone with slated roofs and they fitted easily into the traditional rhythm of the street, their arched ground floors making a pleasant contrast with the other buildings. There have been unfortunate instances of market houses being unnecessarily demolished or crudely altered. This was probably due to ignorance, but in recent years their fine qualities and historical significance are becoming more widely appreciated.

The traditional function of the market house as a centre of major economic activity has long since ceased. Occasionally such houses are used for country markets, but they are more frequently used as district offices, community centres and shops, or they are put to other commercial uses. In the larger towns the central marketing activities did not decline to the same extent. In the late nineteenth century markets erected in the cities have a distinctive architectural character. All the activities took place in a large covered space created by contemporary industrial building techniques, particularly using cast iron and steel. Within this area a great variety of businesses operated. Externally the new market buildings were less severe than industrial buildings. Brick was widely used and there were many architectural refinements such as impressive entrances, mouldings and carvings.

Fairs and markets, for generations an important and interesting aspect of towns, have long since ceased except in a few areas in the west and south-west. They were succeeded by the livestock mart, now a common building type in country towns. Unfortunately all pretence at architecture has disappeared and few marts have any style or presence. This is compounded by the incongruous, even hideous, car parks usually associated with them.

The court-house is another common and traditionally important type of public building. Unlike markets, courts are still conducted in the traditional way, and indeed the whole paraphernalia and mystique surrounding the court-house and its activities has changed little since the last century. It would seem from the comments of some judges that physical comforts inside the buildings have changed little as well. Litigation was always an important aspect of Irish life and the courts were organised on a countrywide basis. Many quite small villages boasted a court-house. Internally the courtroom was distinctive, with its large space formally organised in recognition of

92 Sligo town, Quay Street – town hall. This Venetian-style building provides assembly rooms, municipal offices and initially contained a small market.

93 Cavan town, Town Hall Street – This town hall with its high roof, domestic scale and distinctive windows is a good example of the arts and crafts style.

94 Carrickmacross, Co. Monaghan, New Street – a parochial hall from the turn of the century, a two-storey, gable-fronted building with interesting plasterwork and a distinctive appearance.

95 Naas, Co. Kildare, North Main Street – town hall. This building was adapted from the old jail. The facade treatment, with the emphasis on gables, small windows and so on, is in the arts and crafts tradition.

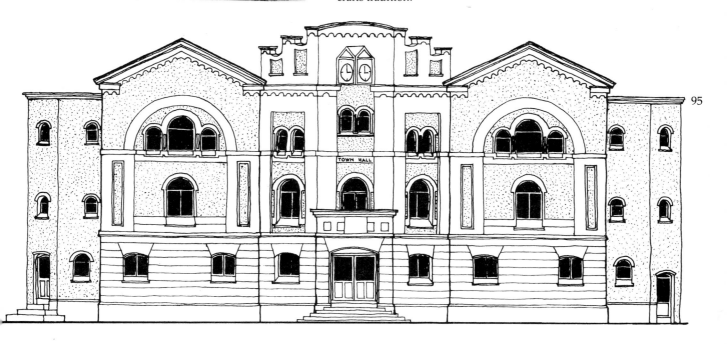

96 Balbriggan, Co. Dublin, George's Square – Carnegie library. This library commands an important position in the street. Built in an unusual Scottish baronial style, its architecture makes it a building of presence in the town.

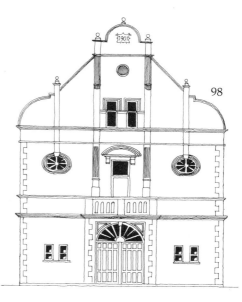

97 Cork city, Patrick Street – Pavilion cinema. This building was erected in the 1920s and is one of a number of distinguished buildings built after the great fire of Cork. The facade is in the classical style with highly decorative tiling. Internally, the building has retained all its essential characteristics with fine plasterwork details in the main auditorium, elegant tearooms, and an impressive entrance foyer.

98 Buncrana, Co. Donegal, upper Main Street – St Mary's Hall. This building is now used as a cinema and community centre. The Art Nouveau style is unusual in a small town.

99 Youghal, Co. Cork, Town Park – bandstand. A fine structure used by the local or visiting band. Elegantly constructed of cast-iron and timber. Many such 'fun buildings' were constructed at the turn of the century during the heyday of the seaside resorts.

100 Kilkenny city, Patrick Street – The City Theatre. An ornate but elegant facade marks the old city theatre. Now a shop, the basic elements of the old theatre are still clearly visible at the rear.

the different participants in the legal drama. The basic requirements were courtrooms, a central hall where much discussion and counselling took place and which was always a centre of activity, jury rooms, judges' and barristers' rooms, with cells and storage areas usually at a lower level. The court-house also provided a meeting place for the grand juries, who were the principal instruments of local administration prior to the establishment of the county councils. Offices and meeting rooms were provided for their purposes. So the interior of the larger court-house was quite complex and allowed scope for imaginative planning. Many court-houses were built in the early nineteenth century and their architecture reflects the classical style popular then. The appearance of the larger ones, although severe in tone, was elegant and impressive with grand porticos and entrances, as if to emphasise the majesty of the law. The smaller court-houses were simpler in design and interior planning, but they aimed at a higher architectural standard than might be considered appropriate in a market house. The concept of the central courtroom still dominated the plan. These court-houses fit neatly into the street, but generally the quality of materials and elegance of design gives even the smallest an air of importance.

Comparatively few court-houses were built from the mid-nineteenth century onwards. Those and the newer ones, such as the court-house in Ballymena, Co. Antrim, are easily recognised by the change in architectural style from the traditional classical to the then more popular Gothic. New courts were also built in Belfast to provide for the High Court and other legal functions as a consequence of the establishment of Northern Ireland as a legal entity. The court-house in Dowra, Co. Cavan – a small village in a remote part of the country – dates from 1932 and is designed with great charm and panache in a classical style common in public buildings of that time. Court-houses were frequently built to a standard plan, and were usually the work of a particular architect with commissions in the same region. The court-houses in a number of County Cork towns – Bantry, Macroom, Kanturk – are obviously by the same designer.

The standard of craftsmanship was high, both in the exterior work, which was usually executed in finely dressed stone, and in the interiors with their handsome pews, judges' benches, and canopies, rather like a Protes-

tant meeting house. The court system remains and is still relatively widespread throughout the country, although many major functions have become centralised. Court-houses are often also the centre of local administration, and their interiors have frequently undergone significant changes, but rarely with any artistic appreciation of the buildings' merit. Where court-houses have retained their original character their interesting interiors should be preserved, if at all possible, even if the buildings need improving in such matters as heating and lighting.

RECREATIONAL BUILDINGS

Although religion, commerce and administration were important aspects of urban life, the need for recreation was not overlooked. Many landlords were responsible for building assembly halls, which became a centre for local entertainment and meetings. These early halls were handsome buildings in the classical style, and were the beginnings of a diverse building type which is still being built today. Their principal feature is the assembly hall where the major gatherings took place – often rooms of elegance and beauty, exhibiting fine plaster-work and other architectural refinements. A few of these early assembly buildings remain and may still provide for recreation of some sort or other, as in Ballinasloe, Co. Galway, Coleraine, Co. Derry, Belfast city and Carlow town. Other such buildings have been put to new uses, some as administrative centres. They are usually marked on the old Ordnance Survey maps[2] as indeed are many other public buildings from this period. Most sizeable towns had an assembly room of some sort, where the local gentry, professional and merchant classes enjoyed themselves. The larger boroughs had civic buildings dating from earlier periods, which usually provided a combination of assembly rooms, council chambers and administrative offices. The great mass of the people, however, were seldom involved, and only rarely would such buildings be found in smaller towns.

Following the Local Government Act of 1898, urban and rural district councils were established. This gave rise to a renewal of local civic pride. Many town halls were erected as centres for the new bodies. They combined the functions of assembly rooms and of administrative offices. The new buildings

101

101

102

102

101 Enniscorthy, Co. Wexford, Castle Street –
the Athenaeum theatre. This theatre has an
impressive classical facade fitting successfully
into the street. It has changed little over the
years. The main assembly room is on the first
floor with meeting rooms underneath.

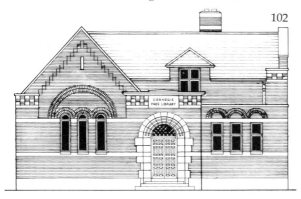

102 Lismore, Co. Waterford, West Street – Carnegie
library. The libraries in the smaller towns fitted neatly
into the local physical structure. They were often no bigger
than dwelling houses. This one was built in a fashion
then common for domestic buildings – neo-Tudor.

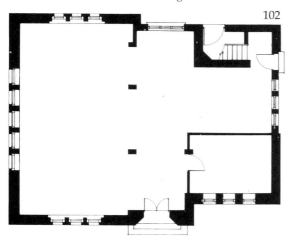

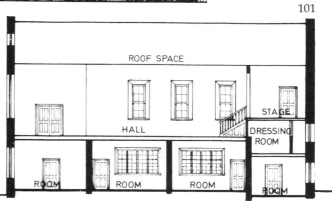

103 This map shows the location of Carnegie Libraries in
Ireland. Most are still in existence and have changed little
externally.

103

were designed in a variety of architectural styles, principally the Gothic or Italianate with occasional examples of the new arts and crafts style, as in Bray, Co. Wicklow, and Cavan town. The interiors were complex but interesting, with the main focus of attention on the entrance hall, council chambers and assembly rooms. The classical style was rare as it was then out of fashion for public buildings.

After the first flush of enthusiasm for local government there was relatively little building in this field. The few local government buildings erected in the twenties and thirties exhibit a modern version of the classical style, which was again becoming popular for public buildings, as in the City Hall in Cork.

The churches were also concerned with the recreational activities of their flocks, and from the late nineteenth century onwards it was fashionable to erect halls for parish activities. Those buildings frequently achieved interesting and at times quite acceptable architectural standards. Their designers were influenced by the architectural fashions of the day, and the buildings are in a localised version of the Art Nouveau or arts and crafts styles and are often gable-fronted with high roofs and attractive plaster-work. Internally they were rather spartan and had few of the facilities now associated with community buildings, perhaps just a few rooms at the back of the stage doubling as dressing rooms and meeting rooms. However, they did attempt to achieve a certain architectural style, at least externally. Because of lack of awareness of the merits of the original buildings many have been crudely modernised in recent times.

Meetings and concerts of all kinds were a popular form of recreation. Other religious and semi-political organisations also built halls – orange halls, masonic halls, Hibernian halls and temperance halls. Architectural styles varied, depending on the finances available and the period in which they were built. Quite a number date from the turn of the century and again the Gothic or arts and crafts styles were popular, but frequently there was no discernible style and the buildings were utilitarian in the extreme, built perhaps of corrugated iron. Even in such cases, however, there was usually a gesture towards architecture, in, for example, the window designs or locally inspired decorative panels.

The live theatre has always been important in urban life. From the eighteenth century onwards, particularly in cities and larger towns, there were purpose-built theatres devoted to the professional entertainment business, opera, concerts and music-hall reviews. Few of these early buildings now remain, although their locations can still be seen on old maps, and in some towns they are part of local folk history. Among the more famous was the Assembly Rooms in Fishamble Street, Dublin, where the first performance of Handel's Messiah was given. During the intervening years the tradition for live entertainment continued, until in this century the advent of radio, cinema, television and the new video industry has all but demolished it. In the late nineteenth century new theatres were erected and older ones refurbished. Improvements in transportation meant that famous players and companies could travel more easily to provincial towns. The audiences were there and the theatrical impressarios investing in buildings invariably put great style and panache into them. As a rule theatres were street buildings, rarely free-standing. A facade might be reticently designed and not very different from the adjacent buildings, perhaps even domestic in character, but there are also quite lavish examples and idiosyncratic interpretations of different architectural styles.

Great care was devoted to the interiors, which were impressive spaces with glittering gilt and brass details and highly ornate and superbly executed plaster-work, unusual in public buildings of the period. Of those that are still standing, the Opera House in Belfast and the Olympia Theatre in Dublin are among the cities' more distinctive buildings. Less famous are the City Theatre in Kilkenny, the bones of which are still clearly evident although its use has changed, and the Athenaeum in Enniscorthy, Co. Wexford, which is still in use and comparatively little changed.

During the early part of this century many theatres were transformed into picture houses, as the first cinemas were called. The changes were often carried out without great damage to their character and some, like the Palace in Cork, are still in use today. However, many are now gone, and others have found a new use not always sympathetic to their character.

Few professional theatres have been erected in recent years with the exception of the Abbey in Dublin and the Opera House in

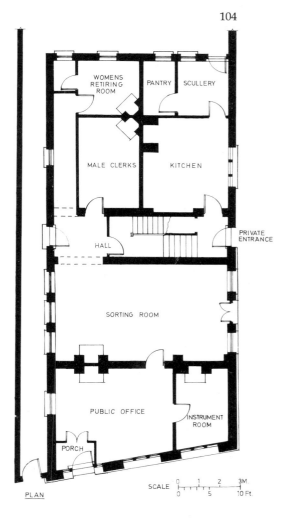

104

PLAN

SCALE

104 Cahir, Co. Tipperary, Church Street – post office. This building, in a gable-fronted Gothic style, also provided living accommodation. Essentially, a small shop, lived over.

105 Belturbet, Co. Cavan, Main Street – post office. Many of the early post-office buildings date from the turn of the century and often had flamboyant fronts.

105

Cork. The trend now, and probably in the future, is towards the erection of purpose-built halls which provide for a range of community recreational facilities. Such halls are often part of building complexes, such as schools and universities. Other public buildings, such as churches and schools, are being transformed into theatres or are put to other entertainment uses. It is important that where theatres exist, whether they are in use as theatres or for other purposes, they should be preserved, and possibly reconverted.

The cinema as a building type made its appearance in the early part of this century. The great era of cinema development was from the twenties onwards. It started in large cities but extended throughout the country until every town of significance boasted a cinema. Initially it was a local hall, which provided accommodation for the travelling cinema operator. Later, as the new medium became popular and commercially successful, purpose-built cinemas were erected. In the larger centres they were on a grand scale and great attention was devoted to the interiors, which, often through exotic plasterwork and paintwork, evoked an image of faraway places, depicting medieval and even Moorish and oriental scenes. The external architecture was somewhat brash, which was perhaps in keeping with the new technology, and cinemas were the first experience many towns had of modernism with its art deco fronts, strip windows and general lack of ornamentation.

The cinema, in contrast to many other modern developments, was usually located in the town centre. It was fitted between shops and houses and the new architecture did not always fit easily into the street. The cinema as a building type lasted only a short time as television, with its unique range and flexibility, was too successful a competitor. Comparatively few cinemas are still in existence. Those that have retained their character evoke nostalgic memories of the thirties and forties.

OTHER PUBLIC BUILDINGS

Libraries have a long-honoured tradition. Mainly associated with larger cities and the more important educational establishments, they did not assume architectural significance in the average town until the latter part of the nineteenth century. Many libraries were built with funds from the Carnegie Trust.[3] They are architecturally varied buildings, the chosen style obviously depending on the individual taste of the architect — Gothic, classical, or a personal interpretation of other historic styles. While many may now be old-fashioned in internal planning, their physical condition is quite sound, and they can be adapted for present-day requirements.

There are other public buildings, not always in every town, and relating principally to the duties of the new local authorities, for example fire stations, wash-houses and occasionally swimming pools. They did not establish any new trends in architecture and the styles again depended on the architect.

For years the extent of new public buildings did not match the scale or the rate achieved at the turn of the century. Public finances were limited and such matters as housing and industry required an ever-increasing share of the finances available. There are buildings of individual interest, but there has been no single period when a comprehensive range of public buildings was erected throughout the country until the recent phase of urban development.

MILITARY ARCHITECTURE

Armies and their activities have always been important in European urban life and Ireland is no exception in this regard. Taking 'the king's shilling' was a common way of securing employment, getting away from the boredom of local life or, in extreme cases, acquiring the necessities to keep body and soul together. The Irish, the Scots and, to a lesser extent, the Welsh have a long tradition of military service. This is partly due to social and economic conditions, and partly to family and local traditions established over many generations. The custom of raising regiments locally contributed to the building of military barracks. Nearly all the campaigns were overseas, but there was always a need for regimental headquarters and local bases. In Ireland there was usually an uneasy relationship between large segments of the population and governments of the day.

Most large towns and many smaller ones have remnants of an old army barracks. The army and its activities played an important part in the nineteenth-century development of some towns, for example Birr, Fermoy, Templemore, Omagh, Enniskillen and Newbridge. The cities were naturally of military significance and army barracks are

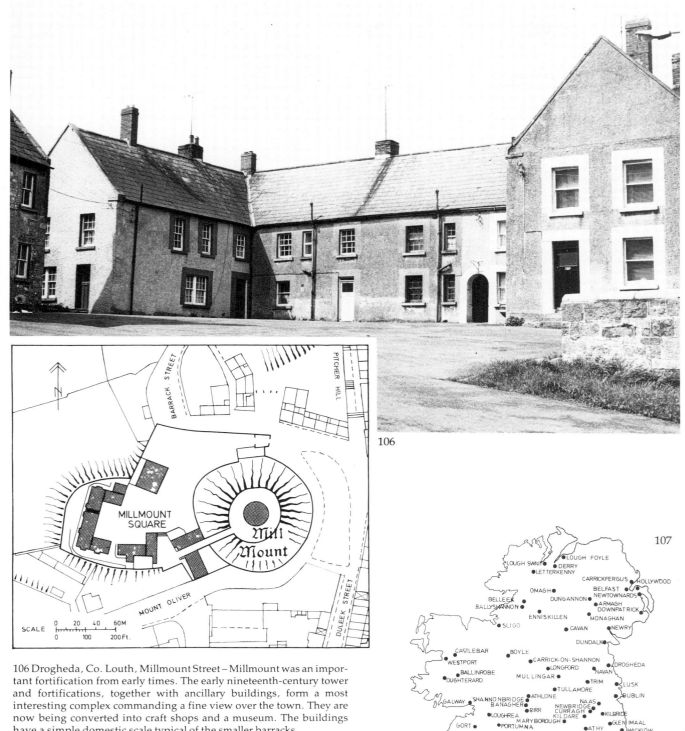

106 Drogheda, Co. Louth, Millmount Street – Millmount was an important fortification from early times. The early nineteenth-century tower and fortifications, together with ancillary buildings, form a most interesting complex commanding a fine view over the town. They are now being converted into craft shops and a museum. The buildings have a simple domestic scale typical of the smaller barracks.

107 This map shows the location of army barracks in the nineteenth century. Some were quite extensive, others small. The physical remnants of such buildings are still to be found. They are of local historical interest and often of architectural and building merit.

to be found in most of them.

The plan and layout of army barracks follows a generally accepted pattern. The buildings are grouped around large open spaces used for drilling and marching, then the commonest type of military training. Many barracks are classical in style with quite a robust and severe expression, and generally with little of the elegance to be found in the great houses of the period. The barracks built later were more ornate and influenced by the fashion for romantic Italianate styles, such as McKee Barracks in Dublin and Ceannt Barracks in the Curragh, Co. Kildare. The layouts were comprehensive, with provision for single and married quarters, religious duties and recreational activities. The army was organised on rigid lines and the layout and internal arrangements of the officers' quarters were much superior to those of the enlisted men. The officers frequently lived outside the barracks and substantial and attractive early-nineteenth-century houses in the military towns were originally built for army officers.

Barracks were generally built of stone, coursed and pointed. The buildings varied in height from two to four storeys. Roofs were of slate and the internal structural work was timber. In many ways they resembled the more utilitarian town houses of the period. Later, as was the fashion, brick was more widely used or occasionally painted stucco work.

In the cities, the major barracks are still being used and to all outward appearance have retained their original character. The requirements of the army have, however, changed tremendously in recent years and there are many internal changes in barracks. Elsewhere, many barracks have become obsolete and are now made over to a variety of uses. Occasionally they are used for reserve forces.

There are also military fortifications and other similar structures which go back to medieval times. Many castles were built with strategic and military considerations in mind. Mostly only remnants of these buildings are extant and they are of historical or archaeological as well as local architectural importance.

The modern police forces were formed in 1867 as the Royal Irish Constabulary, which later evolved into the Garda Síochána and the Royal Ulster Constabulary. The police force was established on a countrywide basis and even remote rural areas had their police barracks. Initially they operated in a time of widespread agitation and unrest and the maintenance of law and order was an important local activity. The policeman, however, was involved in more than law and order. He also acted as the servant of central government in carrying out a whole range of other services. In the days before mass bureaucracy had taken over the local guard was a common sight pushing his bicycle along country roads, serving summonses for such matters as unlighted carts or bicycles and unlicensed dogs and collecting information about population figures and agricultural statistics.

Every town has its constabulary barracks. These buildings are not architecturally unique and by and large they are indistinguishable from the ordinary domestic building. Their requirements were simple – living accommodation, a small office and perhaps another room which might double as a cell and as temporary accommodation for travellers. Initially few new barracks were erected and the accommodation was provided in existing buildings. The average police barracks was essentially a house, large or small depending on the size of the station. As the force developed and as living standards improved it became policy to erect new barracks on a national basis. The typical barracks reflected the traditional vernacular architecture of the day in a slightly classical form similar to many town houses. Married quarters were provided for the sergeant, and the amalgamation of married quarters and barracks requirements has generally been handled with care and success, as in Sneem, Co. Kerry, or Stradbally, Co. Laois, which are examples of a standardised type built by the Board of Works in many small towns since the 1930s. In essence they are well-mannered buildings fitting comfortably into the local environment. Where they are well maintained, and the rural stations particularly have established fine traditions in this regard, they are often among the more attractive buildings in the district.

The coastguard was another arm of the law and in coastal settlements coastguard cottages and stations were erected in the nineteenth century. These buildings usually had a distinctive appearance, although in the local traditional style. Perhaps this is because they are generally in a group set apart from other buildings and usually on a prominent site overlooking the coast. They were single- or two-storey buildings in brick

108 Athlone, Co. Westmeath, Castle Street – a nineteenth-century army barracks developed on the site of earlier fortifications. It forms an important part of the physical structure of the town.

109 Dublin city, Blackhorse Avenue – McKee Barracks, officers' mess. This is an unusually flamboyant army barracks. The buildings are grouped around the vast parade ground. There is a mixture of architectural styles, all executed in brick with superb skill and panache.

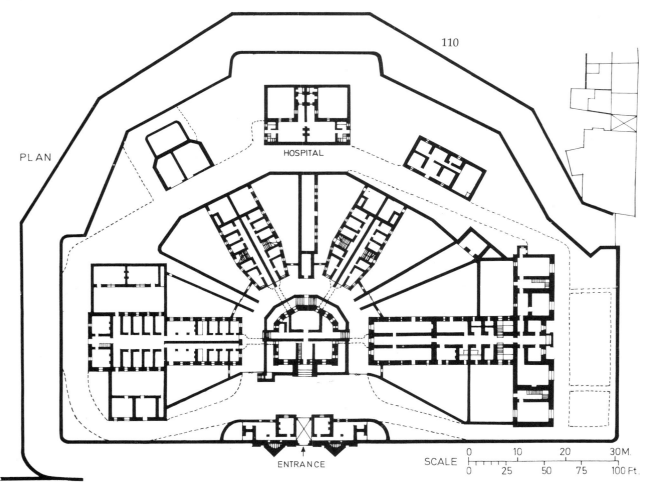

PLAN

HOSPITAL

ENTRANCE

SCALE

0   10   20   30 M.
0   25   50   75   100 Ft.

110

110 Carlow town, Kennedy Avenue – jail. The plan illustrates the typical layout of a nineteenth-century jail. Remnants of this building can still be observed, particularly its impressive entrance.

111

112

113

111 Prototype garda station. This small garda station (Finnea, Co. Westmeath, Main Street), similar to many erected in the 1950s throughout the country, would fit neatly into any village or small town. It provided administrative accommodation and also living space for one officer – usually the local sergeant. Some larger stations of the same period were two-storey in the same simple classical style.

112 Tarbert, Co. Kerry, Harbour Road – the Bridewell. A small local jail, not now used, but worthy of attention for the quality of its stonework and, of course, for its historical significance.

113 Nenagh, Co. Tipperary, Castle Street – former governor's house of Nenagh jail; an impressive building, perhaps indicative of the status of such a position.

114, 115 Dublin city, Buckingham Street 114 and Thomas Street 115 – fire stations. These buildings fit successfully into the street pattern. It would be difficult to achieve this today as more complex provisions have to be made, for example, car parking and ease of access.

or stone with slated roofs. Coastguard activities have been centralised to a large extent now, as have many other maritime activities, and so coastguard stations are often now ordinary dwelling-houses, but as a general rule they have retained their charm and character.

In the nineteenth century, prisons were erected in many of the larger provincial centres. As might be expected, they were built with security and safety in mind. The architecture was robust without any frills, though the entrance was designed to create an impression of permanence and authority. A principal feature was the prison wall, which was built in stone as were the other buildings, and even today the wall may be an important element in the surrounding environment. Staff housing was frequently provided adjacent to the prison. It consisted of single- and two-storey houses, never very large and providing minimum requirements. They were similar to staff houses provided by other bodies, and often are in a faintly Gothic style. The prison service has been centralised to a large extent, and in many provincial towns the prisons are now occupied for other uses, as centres of admin-istration, for industry, or similar activity. In Carlow town and Tullamore the old jails are now industrial concerns, in Dundalk the jail is now used partly as a Garda barracks, in Wexford town the jail has been turned into county council offices and in Downpatrick the old jail is now being converted into a museum. In all cases the buildings retain their traditional prison appearance, especially in the surrounding wall and impressive entrances.

Notes

[1] An interesting account of the building of the work-houses is given in 'The Building of the Workhouse', P. J. Meghen in *Administration*, Volume 3, No. 1, Spring 1955.

[2] The old large scale Ordnance Survey maps for towns, many of which can be examined in the National Library, Dublin, and the Public Records Office, Belfast, contain much interesting and fascinating information about towns often difficult to obtain elsewhere. For example, the internal plans of many public buildings were indicated and also garden layouts.

[3] Andrew Carnegie was a Scotsman, who emigrated to America, established a great industrial and financial empire, and then spent considerable sums of money setting up libraries and other cultural buildings in Britain and Ireland.

116

116 Portlaoise Co. Laois, Dublin Road – general hospital. This building, with its flat roof, clean lines, lack of ornamentation and horizontal emphasis, is an important early example of the modern style. It did not acknowledge any traditional influences. A good example of the style, well executed, it still looks impressive today.

Chapter Six

Commercial Buildings

The commonest type of town is the market centre, which provides a comprehensive commercial and administrative service over a wide area. The social developments and tremendous increase in the rural population of the early nineteenth century had significant effects on the economic structure of towns, which to a large extent still exist today. The towns developed to provide a service and marketing function for the country population. A small town with a population of no more than a thousand may have up to twenty shops, a couple of banks, certain professional services and administrative and miscellaneous functions.

The typical village has a single main street where practically every building is a shop of some sort. There are butchers, drapers, grocers, hardware shops and, of course, public houses. Shops, particularly in the smaller villages, may provide three or four services in the same establishment. The classic example is the pub situated at the back of the grocery, which also sells a little bit of hardware, drapery and the local newspapers. When dropping in for a drink you can also buy a shirt, a pair of boots, or a spade or shovel. The commercial importance of the Irish town has given rise to one of the great glories of local architecture, the traditional shop and more specifically the shopfront.

Take a stroll down the main street of any small town or village. If you are already familiar with its charm and character you will no doubt be looking out for the traditional shopfronts, perhaps a new type to add to your personal recollection. If, however, local architecture does not yet mean anything special to you, then take a look at the shop-fronts. There will be an exciting and unique visual experience in store for you. Do it soon because good shops are unfortunately becoming rare in our towns. In any classification of European local architecture the Irish shopfront must surely rank high as an example of local craftsmanship and artistic achievement.

The traditional shop which we see today is generally a late nineteenth- or early twentieth-century development. There are few shopfronts remaining from the beginning of modern urban development in the eighteenth or early nineteenth centuries. There are occasionally shops which are obviously extremely old with authentic early nineteenth-century windows, clay tile floors and simple fittings. Their survival is remarkable but they are now rarely busy. They may have reverted to residential use and this may have helped to ensure their preservation. The early shopfronts which can be seen in old prints were small in scale and the services provided were of a personal nature. The use of classical details was quite common, as would be expected. Display windows were small, however, influenced by the glass sizes readily available.

Although comparatively little actual urban expansion took place during the late nineteenth century, many existing premises were improved. Living standards and requirements were continually rising and new technological developments, such as plate glass and cast iron, allowed greater flexibility in shop planning and layout. Perhaps the greatest spur to improvement was the business drive and acumen of a particular individual who, having inherited the firm, was anxious to impress their own style and personality on it, or who had worked their way up from apprentice to charge-hand and at last achieved the ambition of owning their own shop.

Commercial activities are never static especially not shopping: even today it is in continual change. Fortunately at the turn of the century the high quality of existing architecture was maintained. Although businesses were improved, the classical style was continued but with greater boldness and verve, using traditional details and motifs, such as columns, cornices and fasciae. Extremely ornate shopfronts were also built for more prosperous businesses, with intricate plaster mouldings, polished granite columns with highly decorative caps, cut stone trim to windows and doors and the highest quality joinery. Internally the same high standards would be carried through with the fittings specially made for the particular project. Many of the best shops date from this period.

The high standard of building continued through the twenties and thirties, and up to the fifties a consistently high standard of design was maintained. In the thirties and forties, chromium, tile and vitrolite fronts became popular and, although modern in style compared to the earlier ones, these fronts retained a sense of scale, and a concern for detailing. As late as the 1950s, improvements to shops, particularly in the smaller town, were still carried out with sensitivity and care. Although the old timber fasciae and columns were replaced, the use of traditional motifs and signs was continued but executed in plaster. Instead of hand-painted lettering, individual block letters were made. This was a simple but effective method of making the best use of the techniques and materials available, an example of local architecture at its best.

Over the years certain styles have become associated with different trades, for example drapery shops, particularly the more prosperous, were elegantly designed with large windows divided by slender columns and arches. Watchmakers are fond of gold lettering against the background of a dark facade. Chemists, successors to the old apothecaries, have a crisp and clinical appearance. Butchers have traditionally used tiles with animal motifs as features. The ubiquitous public house embraces a wide variety of architectural styles – the details are sturdy and the lettering intricate. The traditional pub fronts are often among the best buildings in the street. In small villages, the shops have simple but dignified expressions and usually an entire facade is picked out in a strong colour with simply carved wooden details, an indication that the shopkeeper appreciated good style, although the requirements of his business or his financial situation did not allow for a more ornate approach. He will, however, have his name displayed in bold and clear lettering. All shop types have one thing in common – a feeling for design. They have an essential beauty and order which is timeless, and which has nothing to do with age or function. So many modern shops are garish and ugly that the average person has come to associate beauty with age, and this is at the root of the current fashion for pastiche architecture.

Names are important elements in the traditional shopfront. They identify a family with its own distinctive tradition. A family that has been trading in a town for generations will usually take pride in the name over the shop. It proclaims that they are not another branch of a faceless multiple but a shop whose name is respected and whose service is appreciated.

When examined in detail, shopfronts reveal many architectural delights and some idiosyncracies as well. In the smaller shops there are the simple classical columns made in timber and interpreted according to local traditions. The bigger shops will have more ornate details, such as hand-carved Ionic and Corinthian capitals executed in stone by craftsmen working from a pattern book. Lettering includes many variations of classical and other alphabets. In some districts it is possible to distinguish the trademark of a master craftsman, who gives an individual flourish to certain letters. The lettering and signs usually respect the architectural style of the buildings and as a result even the smallest lettering can be read without any difficulty. It may only be a question of glass embossing or relating the sign to the proportion of the doors and windows. Another feature is the marvellous and uninhibited use of strong colours which are not out of any textbook. The strongest colours are usually relieved by contrasting tones for the smaller details, and, in particular, the use of white for windows. When situated at the end of a street or on a corner, a boldly painted building can give added character to the entire area.

The shopfront is also of educational value as indeed is the whole range of local archi-

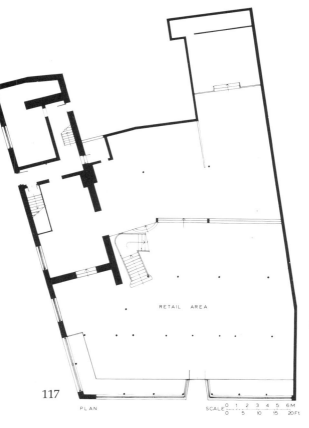

PLAN

SCALE 0 1 2 3 4 5 6M
0 5 10 15 20Ft

117

117

117 Sligo town, Wine Street – Lyons & Co. An early provincial example of the department store. The large interior spaces, built around a cast-iron structure, facilitated the multi-department concept. The facade, however, respected the scale of the street and surrounding buildings.

118

119

118 Dundalk, Co. Louth, Clanbrassil Street – Dearey's shopfront has a spacious and elegant appearance, traditionally associated with drapers.

119 Abbeyleix, Co. Laois, Main Street – Morrissey's. This shop, which dates from the late nineteenth century and replaced an earlier shop, has changed little. It shows an elegant use of classical details finely executed in timber, with good block lettering. The interior, which is unusually spacious, is most exciting and incorporates a pub and grocery with robust and interesting fittings – a fine country version of the more opulent city shops.

tecture. Even the simplest front can act as an introduction to architecture and aesthetics. In drawing or photographing local shops, maybe belonging to their parents or a relative, schoolchildren can learn about architectural styles, and become aware of such matters as colour, design and proportion; features that are part and parcel of the western architectural tradition can be observed and studied in one's own street.

The interior planning of shops is also of significance and interest, although interiors are usually overlooked and underestimated in comparison with the more colourful and now widely appreciated facades. The traditional pub is warm and cosy, full of nooks and crannies, where all sorts of important decisions might be made, local or world controversies solved, familiar stories retold. Frequently pub interiors achieved extremely high design and constructional standards, the warmth of mahogany in the counters, partitions and panelling with exquisite hand-carved details contrasting with highly polished brass fittings and glittering mirrors. It is obvious that the same care and attention was devoted to the interior as to the facade. Drapers' shops were airy and graceful, creating the best conditions for display. Chemists' shops full of medicinal smells, displayed medicines and goods in exotic jars in exquisitely made glass-fronted cabinets.

The department store is a relatively new concept in shopping. Within one building many services were provided – in a way they were like the old village store – although traditionally the department store has been associated with clothing and household goods. Today they sell everything. The new department stores coincided with the development of modern architecture; and interior planning and construction utilised modern techniques, such as structural steel, lifts and large plate-glass windows. However, the modern influence was often modified by the application of historical details, never in the purest way but with the freedom associated with the early modernists. Some of these first department stores remain and have retained to a large extent their external character: Robinson Cleavers in Donegall Square, Belfast, Burtons in Dame Street, Dublin, Austins in The Diamond, Derry city, Moons in Galway city and Lyons in Sligo town are still among the more interesting commercial buildings in their respective towns. Internally, however, some have been changed significantly. The department stores

were usually three storeys high, all used for retailing, unlike the traditional shop where only the ground floor was used.

Shopping patterns are continually changing. Change in itself is never bad, but when accompanied by a lack of sensitivity and appreciation for architectural quality or local character it can be disastrous and over the past two decades disastrous things have happened to the traditional shops, all in the name of progress. Dignified fasciae have been ripped out and replaced by crude timber sheeting and imitation stonework, and elaborate and sensitive hand-painted or carved lettering has been removed and replaced by mass-produced plastic names and signs. Entire interiors of rare beauty and quality have been removed because the shopkeeper felt it was old-fashioned or perhaps because his or her neighbour did the same. Occasionally, modern embellishments have been laid over the existing fasciae and the traditional details can still be seen. Unfortunately in other cases the existing facades were completely removed or destroyed. These so-called improvements have occurred everywhere in large towns and small villages. In some provincial centres the traditional shopfront has become a rarity because of the growth of the multiple store, the spread of new commercial ideas in retailing and advertising influenced by American patterns and the lack of understanding and respect for architectural styles. Multiple stores have been accused of imposing their own image irrespective of the local character, but even local shopkeepers, who should appreciate and value individuality and distinctiveness, often replaced their traditional shopfront with a modern one, which follows a mass rather than a personal style. By and large, the new fronts have completely ignored the great traditions of their predecessors. It is rare to find a sensitively designed modern shopfront.

Local names, which were a feature of towns for generations, also suffered in the quest for modernisation: Patrick Burke was replaced by The High Chapparral, and Tom O'Connor by The Wagon Wheel. A mid-Atlantic culture was taking over and at a high architectural price. The loss of fine shopfronts is a sad chapter in Irish architectural history.

Fortunately, there is a movement within the last few years against this senseless destruction. This has happened partly as a reaction against the sheer banality and ugli-

120 Mullingar, Co. Westmeath, Market Street – Shaw's. This shopfront shows the fine craftwork of traditional fronts.
121 Downpatrick, Co. Down, English Street – butcher's shop. An exotic shopfront carried out in tiles and incorporating distinctive emblems and motifs.

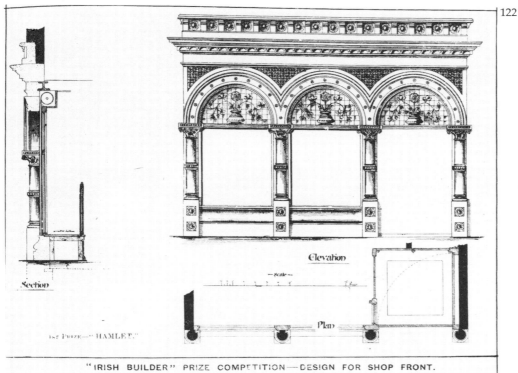

Section

Elevation

— Scale —

Plan

1st Prize—"HAMLET."

"IRISH BUILDER" PRIZE COMPETITION—DESIGN FOR SHOP FRONT.

122 Shopfronts – the first prize in a shopfront competition promoted by *The Irish Builder* at the turn of the century. The drawing illustrates the exuberance and vitality of shopfront design at this period. The best quality materials and the highest standard of craftsmanship were the norm. Many shopfronts like this were erected, particularly in the larger towns. Far too many have been lost.

ness of the modern shopfront and, let us hope, is partly due to a growing appreciation of local architecture and its importance to the cultural life of the community. It is now popular to simulate the old shopfronts with olde worlde lettering and imitation Georgian windows. However, the new designs do not match up to the original in either craftsmanship or design: the recreation of traditional designs in an acceptable way demands scholarship and commitment to the idea. Otherwise, it is preferable to use a modern design which is sympathetic in scale and materials to its surroundings. Many shopkeepers can now be compared to the householder who was prepared almost to give away to the travelling trader valuable old brasses and furniture. Suddenly they are valuable, but unlike household antiques, it is not possible to buy them back, so they try to recreate the originals – a poor substitute.

BANK BUILDINGS

The banking system in Ireland developed in the nineteenth century, although the best known institution, the Bank of Ireland, was established as early as 1782. Banks are all involved in the process of taking in deposits and lending out money and so they are the successors of the Renaissance financiers of Florence and the other European financial centres. This significantly influenced the architectural qualities of the first bank buildings. Banks had to exude an atmosphere of stability, prosperity, permanence and honesty. Bank buildings, therefore, have always imparted style and dignity to the street in which they are situated. The banks extended rapidly throughout the country during the nineteenth century. Most provincial towns had a number of banks and even quite small towns might have one or two establishments. They usually adopted the most significant and fashionable architectural styles of the period. Certain styles were popular with different banks, partly because these styles were popular at the date of the bank's establishment. For example, Bank of Ireland buildings are usually in the classical style, which is consistent with an institution established in the eighteenth century. The National Bank, founded by Daniel O'Connell and others in 1834, also favoured classical architecture, as at Ballymahon, Co. Longford, and Dun Laoghaire, Co. Dublin. The Northern Bank and the Provincial Bank, both founded in the 1820s,

also favoured the classical, but more particularly for their earlier branches. Other banks established later in the nineteenth century, such as the Royal Bank and the Munster and Leinster Bank, favoured the then fashionable Gothic style and also the Venetian and Italianate styles, which are always considered appropriate for banks.

The most prestigious architects were employed and no effort was spared as regards the quality of materials, craftsmanship and accommodation provided. Facades were often executed in finely dressed stone, with elaborately carved mouldings and details. The interiors were equally impressive: high-ceilinged banking halls, with ornate and impressive plaster-work, handsome timber fittings and sumptuous marble floors were all designed to impress and at times overwhelm the customers. A bank would not easily be mistaken for an ordinary shop or dwelling. At the same time, their general proportions, use of materials, adherence to building and roof lines, did show a regard for other buildings in the street.

The administrative organisation of the banks at this time fitted into the social structure of the average town – like the shopkeeper, the bank manager lived over the shop, so to speak, and these early banks were not only commercial buildings but town dwellings as well. In smaller towns the commercial aspect was secondary to the living accommodation provided for the manager. It was important for him not only to live in style but to be seen to do so. It was part of the mystique which the banks were obviously anxious to create. The bank buildings are usually the most prestigious and architecturally interesting commercial buildings. They gave a sense of dignity and presence to the streets in which they were located and they are important elements in local architectural heritage.

Since their establishment, the banks have been expanding and developing in accordance with economic trends. Over the years new premises were built or older ones renewed. Architectural styles were varied, reflecting current attitudes, but a consistently high standard of design and craftsmanship was maintained, demonstrating the importance the banking companies then attached to architectural standards.

The banking system underwent a radical reorganisation in the 1960s, which heralded a new phase of rationalisation and development, but which had unfortunate conse-

123

124

125

126

123 Ballymena, Co. Antrim, Bridge Street – Woolworth's. This shows the simple but handsome style adopted by Woolworth's. Multiple organisations can, if they wish, maintain high design standards and yet exhibit a 'brand image'. This is a good shopfront by any standards – simple and clear timber lettering, bright but restrained fascia and elegant, curved glass fronts.

124 Dublin city, Dame Street – Burton's. This flamboyant building is an example of an early-modern office and shop development. Extremely large windows with decorative tiled finish on what is probably a steel structure. Influenced by the Art Nouveau style.

125 Cork city, Patrick Street – Cash's. Cash's was rebuilt in the 1920s following the great fire. Its subtle

curves are matched by the restrained but distinctive classical style. The rebuilding of Patrick Street in Cork resulted in many new buildings of a high standard. If this rebuilding had taken place in the 1960s the results would probably have been disastrous (compare Cash's with Todd's of Limerick, for example).

126 Westport, Market Street – Tylers. Another example of a good-quality shopfront from a chain store.

127

127 Dundalk, Co. Louth, Dundalk Street – corner shop, pub and grocery. This shop is incorporated successfully into a group of small brick houses originally built by a local brewery.

quences architecturally. The first casualty was the individuality of the various banks. Traditionally the bank names had been incorporated with the buildings as an integral part of the architecture, often exquisitely hand-carved in stone or finely made bronze lettering. These were replaced by a standard plastic sign which was fitted to all buildings regardless of the visual effects. Of more lasting concern, however, are the architectural standards of the new bank buildings. Some existing buildings were considered unsuitable for new banking techniques, and in addition many new buildings were required because of economic and social improvements. Somehow the same malaise which affected the shopkeepers also affected the banks. The new buildings largely ignored the great traditions established by their predecessors. Following the then current trends in architecture little consideration was given to the other buildings in the street. Banks were often brash and insensitively designed, although still opulently conceived and constructed of the most expensive materials. The social concept of the bank had also changed. The new buildings were rarely residential – the bank manager like the shopkeepers, had moved out and now lived in a private house on the outskirts of the town – and the new banks in smaller villages were usually single-storey flat-roofed buildings, which might be mistaken for the local public convenience except that the windows were made of bronze. The banks had declined drastically and the fine classical and Gothic essays of earlier days were a memory.

OFFICES

The growth of service employment is a distinctive feature of modern society, although its beginnings go back a hundred years or more, influenced by administrative and financial developments on the one hand – the development of the joint stock company, the concept of insurance, the growth of public and government institutions – and on the other hand by technological developments – the invention of the typewriter and carbon copying, which brought a revolution in clerical work, the use of structural steel and the development of the lift, which radically changed building forms. Offices are the building type which, in recent years, has shaped the development of city centres more than any other. If shops were the most common commercial building types in previous generations, then offices certainly are today. Historically the modern office development began in the latter part of the nineteenth century, and its development has continued ever since with periodic lulls. As a rule offices are located in cities and occasionally larger provincial centres. It is only in recent years that the purpose-built office as distinct from the public authority building was located in smaller towns. As such it is not yet an important building type in the average town.

Initially the main impetus for office development was through activities such as insurance, shipping, banking, building societies and, later on, State departments. These organisations were involved in financial dealings of various sorts with the public, and, as with the banks, an impression of trustworthiness and an air of prosperity were required.

Perhaps more than with most other building types, there is no specific style which can be associated with offices. There are variations of classical, Gothic, Venetian and others, depending on the architects' and clients' tastes. The common aim was perhaps to achieve a high quality of design and craftsmanship both externally and internally. It was essentially a free style often using historic architectural details in a personalised way to provide an individually pleasant composition. There were relatively few isolated buildings as the terrace was, in the early part of the twentieth century, still the accepted form in city and town centres. There was little need to provide for such present-day requirements as car parking.

Early office development coincided with the beginnings of modern architecture, a principal feature of which is lack of ornamentation, a more restrained elevational appearance, and a greater emphasis on windows rather than solid walls. Some early office blocks have a distinctly modern air with large expanses of glass and a mere indication of architectural details as at Booth's Cycle Agency (later Pneumatic Tyre Co. – where the first pneumatic tyre was produced) St Stephen's Street, Dublin. It is in the present phase of development, which began in the sixties, that the truly modern glass fronted type of office block began to make a major impact on our cities and towns. The first phase of office development possibly existed from the 1890s to the 1920s. The few office blocks of the thirties were often State

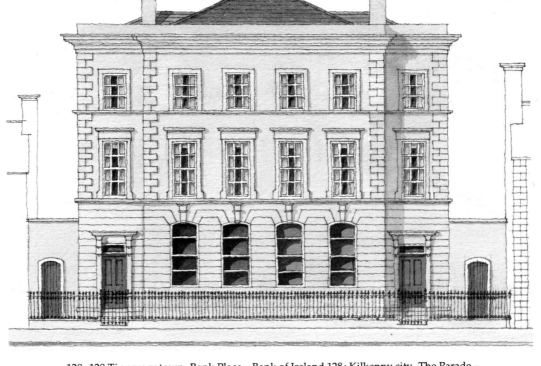

128, 129 Tipperary town, Bank Place – Bank of Ireland 128; Kilkenny city, The Parade – Bank of Ireland 129. These drawings show two bank buildings of impressive scale and design. Although they would never be mistaken for dwelling houses they do relate well to the nearby buildings. Originally they would have provided living accommodation also.

129

130 Dublin, D'Olier Street – an early office block with a highly individualistic facade. The varied roof shapes and gable fronts are enriched by the patterned brick-work. Such buildings, especially when they are in prominent positions, often assume a personality of their own. D'Olier Street and Dublin would miss this building should it go as many others have done.

131 Newry, Co. Down, Hill Street – Northern Bank. Bank buildings were often influenced by popular styles. This Gothic-style building probably reflects the architect's own taste but its strong expression would be acceptable to a bank.

132 Dublin city, Stephen Street – an early-modern office block. Not quite the bland facade of later developments. Also, it respects the street line.

inspired and a modified classical style was common.

HOTELS

Hotels in the modern sense began with the improvements in transportation in the eighteenth and nineteenth centuries, that is the development of the canals, railways and coaching systems. The development of hotels was an integral part of the new transportation business, as many journeys required an overnight stay. Many towns had an hotel or inn of some sort, which was generally indistinguishable from the more substantial houses or business premises of the town, and the proprietor often combined inn-keeping with other activities.

As the need for more facilities became evident, many older hotels were improved. The country town hotel, by incorporating adjacent premises, extended along the street without destroying the rhythm of the facade. Others declined or went out of business altogether.

The canal hotels were built in a pleasant classical style, and in their prime provided accommodation of a high quality, although different to what we might expect today. Most towns served by canals would have some such buildings, but few remain today and fewer still as hotels. In Robertstown, Co. Kildare, the canal hotel is used as a banqueting and community centre, and was rescued from obvious neglect and decay by an enthusiastic local committee. At Portobello Bridge in Dublin the old Canal Hotel, after being a nursing home for many years, has been tastefully restored and is now an office-block. Unfortunately an equally impressive building in Tullamore was demolished a few years ago despite the protests of concerned local enthusiasts.

The railways, and the consequent development of the seaside resort, gave a dramatic impetus to hotel building in towns such as Bray, Bangor and Portrush. Frequently the new resort hotels were buildings of presence and quality, commanding prominent sites. Hotels such as the Slieve Donard in Newcastle, Co. Down, the Great Southern in Galway, and the Queen's Hotel in Bangor were more akin to the great houses of the past than to the ordinary commercial inn. The railway companies built hotels with the same architectural care as they build stations, but not always echoing the 'house style' of the particular company.

Purpose-built hotels, usually located in the cities or large resorts, had a different architectural character from the ordinary commercial hotel. They were more flamboyant in appearance and were architecturally quite demonstrative. They made extensive use of intricate plaster- and iron-work. The styles varied from Gothic to Italianate. They had elaborate and ornate elevational treatments, with vigorous use of traditional building materials – brick, stone and plaster. The interiors, particularly the entrance hall and main public rooms, were impressive in their conception and execution – elaborate staircases, high-class joinery, unusual and artistic tiling – all designed to create a sense of well-being, style, opulence and comfort for the visitor. The Imperial Hotel in Cork City is still as architecturally impressive as ever and, in spite of internal modernisation, retains its old atmosphere.

Many nineteenth-century hotels are now gone. In the cities they were demolished to make way for new office blocks or residential development; in the traditional holiday resorts, they have declined from their previous glamour and style to become ordinary public houses or apartments. Those that remain have frequently been changed out of all recognition. Like the public houses, many have retained their facades, but have replaced their splendid interiors, perhaps to provide more modern services, but certainly at a loss of architectural quality and distinctiveness.

133 Kilkenny city, Parliament Street – Lennon's. A restrained but elegant facade built in brick and painted. The shopfront is timber with simple classical details. Again, large windows to facilitate display but which fit successfully into the street.

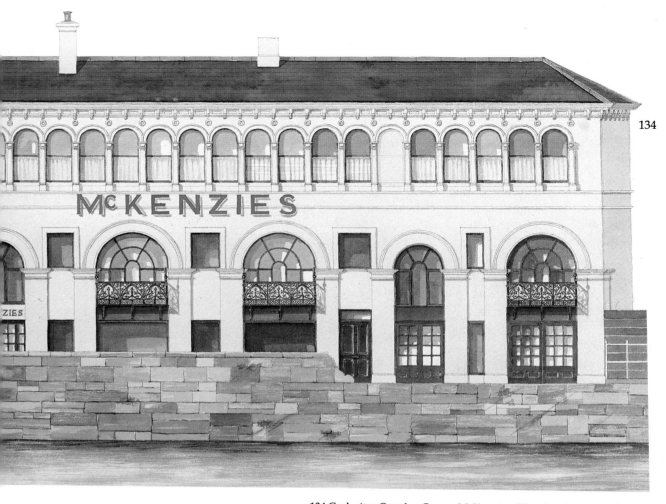

134 Cork city, Camden Quay – McKenzies. This shop faces onto the quay. In a distinctive Italian style, with finely proportioned facades, good plaster and ironwork details, it was built in the late 1920s and still is a hardware and general merchant store. It was extended in the late 1940s in a manner exactly repeating the original.

135 Ballydehob, Co. Cork, Main Street.

135

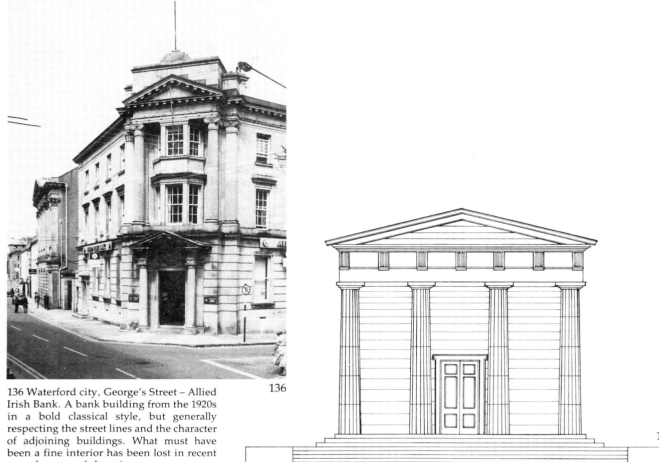

136 Waterford city, George's Street – Allied Irish Bank. A bank building from the 1920s in a bold classical style, but generally respecting the street lines and the character of adjoining buildings. What must have been a fine interior has been lost in recent years because of alterations.

137 Limerick, Glentworth Street – Savings Bank in the Greek style, with an impressive portico – more like a public building than the traditional bank.

136

1

138

138 Sligo town, Stephen Street – Ulster Bank. This bank building commands an important position in the town and is built in an Italianate style – the classic 'merchant's palace'.

139 Newcastle, Co. Down – Slieve Donard Hotel. This old photograph from the Lawrence Collection captures the atmosphere typical of many of the hotels built in the great age of railways.

140 Carnlough, Co. Antrim, Marina Road – a small commercial hotel, built in 1912. Its idiosyncratic facade reflects the style and features of the arts and crafts movement.

141 Glengarriff, Co. Cork, Bantry Road – the Eccles Hotel. Built to cater for the tourist industry this building has a simple facade. The balcony and porch, however, distinguish it from the general house, and this is further emphasised by pleasant interior spaces.

142 Belfast city, Great Victoria Street – Robinson's Bar. An impressive facade with fine plaster mouldings and good shopfront, usually overshadowed by its more famous neighbour, the Crown Liquor Saloon. Robinson's however, is a building of quality with an interesting interior in the pub tradition of a large room divided into intimate spaces.

Chapter Seven

Industry and Transport

INDUSTRIAL BUILDINGS

A popular view of Ireland is of a traditional agricultural economy rapidly developing into a modern industrial society. This image suggests that there are few examples of industrial buildings with their origins in the industrial revolution or before. Except in north-east Ulster there was undoubtedly no great concentration of industries. Nevertheless the cities, larger towns and many medium-sized towns all have industrial buildings, many of which are of architectural and social interest, and particularly in a local context.

Modern industry with the workplace separate from the dwelling, began in the late eighteenth century, but its main impact was felt throughout the nineteenth century. The industrial revolution changed the face of many European countries and large parts of North America. In Ireland the main impact was in Ulster, particularly in the Lagan and Bann valleys, and its most obvious effect was the tremendous growth of Belfast. Outside Ulster industry was based on traditional activities – brewing, distilling, milling, cloth manufacture and engineering – catering principally for a local market. Many firms were family-run and operated in both commerce and industry: most have disappeared through time, although they have left physical traces.

The process of industrialisation forms part of the economic and social growth of the country. Industries were established to provide for the needs of a growing population. There was little emphasis on export, which was mainly of agricultural products. An important aspect of industry is its contin-

tinuous change and rationalisation. The mills and workshops of the nineteenth century superseded the home-based crafts and smaller industries of an earlier period. This in essence is the process of rationalisation, which is still continuing today. For example, many earlier grain mills were adapted to provide for the needs of the developing textile industry. The Irish parliament of the late eighteenth century (Grattan's Parliament) gave grants for building and improving mills and factories.

The form of industrial buildings is influenced by the needs of technology more than many other building types. It is difficult to envisage a modern plant operating in a multistorey building but several storeys were often a feature of early industrial buildings. The style and appearance of these early industrial buildings is often quite different from the residential, commercial and public buildings of the same period elsewhere in the town, although the materials used were similar: stone walls, timber floors and slated roofs.

There are various types of industrial buildings, ranging from the mill with the miller's house attached, which might be no bigger than many countryside houses, to the large textile mills in the towns of Ulster and the big breweries and distilleries in cities. The architectural appearance of the buildings also varies. The smaller buildings were simple and somewhat severe in appearance, built of stone with slated roofs, with perhaps brick trim around the windows as the only decoration. The larger buildings were often quite ornate, built in brick and stone with diverse architectural details: columns, cornices, ornamental doorways and windows.

Early industrial buildings lacked architectural styles in the traditional sense. Even in the late nineteenth century, when the stylistic approach to architecture was popular, industrial buildings rarely tried to copy Gothic structures or classical temples, although frequently historical details were included as embellishments in more prosperous buildings, such as Bannatyne's Mill, now Ranks, in Limerick city. They were conceived as buildings primarily to house complex and often fascinating machines. The smaller buildings were often fitted into the street scene without any great disruption of rhythm or proportion. The site area was relatively limited; it would have been no greater than ordinary commercial premises.

The larger undertakings were usually concentrated into clearly defined areas, perhaps close to the river, and today such areas include a variety of buildings, ranging from the old nineteenth-century warehouses to modern industrial sheds. In the seaports they were located adjacent to the harbour.

Structurally they represented a new departure from traditional building methods. For the first time multi-storey buildings were provided which had to carry heavy loads and allow for complex activities on the upper floors. The industrial process had a vertical emphasis and each activity was carried out on a different level. The buildings were compact in area but were often five or six storeys high. They must have made a tremendous impression when first built and even today these buildings are among the most impressive structures in the smaller towns. They also pioneered the use of cast-iron for structural purposes and there are many examples of interesting and intricate constructional techniques using this new material. Compared to modern buildings they were rather narrow as, until the use of structural steel was developed in the late nineteenth century, it was difficult to roof over large spans. The stone walls and timber floors were massively constructed to carry the weight of the machinery and its vibrations. As a result many are still structurally sound today despite being underused or empty for years. Others have been adapted for present-day uses as community buildings or residential accommodation. Few are still used for their original purposes.

Industrial architecture has not been widely appreciated except, appropriately enough, in Ulster, where E. R. Green's pioneer survey in *Industrial Archaeology of County Down* (Belfast 1963) was the first systematic attempt to evaluate the heritage of industrial architecture. Surveys of the remaining counties in Northern Ireland have recently been completed by Dr Alan McCutcheon in *Industrial Archaeology of Northern Ireland* (Belfast 1980). The Ulster Folk Museum, which has re-erected a spade mill as part of its collection, is also doing much to foster a wider interest in industrial architecture. The work in Ulster is now beginning to arouse interest elsewhere in the country. Recent development plans and architectural surveys are now recognising the historical and architectural importance of industrial buildings.

Until the early part of this century multi-storeyed industrial buildings were still being constructed, and basic designs had changed little over the years. There was then a relative lull in industrial development. The next major phase was in the 1930s when a programme of industrial development was commenced to provide alternative employment for the large numbers leaving agriculture and to reduce unemployment levels which were then severe during the depression. They were the first examples of modern industrial buildings as we know them today.

The architectural concept had changed radically from the nineteenth century. The source of power had also changed – water power was by then almost a folk memory – steam and, even more so, electricity were the energy sources. Industries were on the outskirts of towns rather than in the centre, principally because of the influence of motor transport. The use of new building techniques – structural steel and concrete – allowed more flexible building systems and large areas could be roofed giving clear internal spaces. The typical industrial building of this period has a two-storey front with a comparatively large single-storey building behind. The functional tradition had now declined and factories began to look more and more like public buildings: classical motifs in columns and mouldings and classical-style windows were quite popular as ornamentation. These industrial buildings still retained a certain distinctive quality. One particularly interesting feature is the north light roof truss designed expressly to obtain good lighting on the factory floor, but which also has resulted in interesting roof profiles. Many older buildings were also adapted and modified during this phase of industrial development, seldom, however,

143

143 Kilbeggan, Co. Westmeath – Locke's Distillery, a remnant of a past industrial age. Many such buildings are still structurally sound and have potential for a wide variety of uses.

144

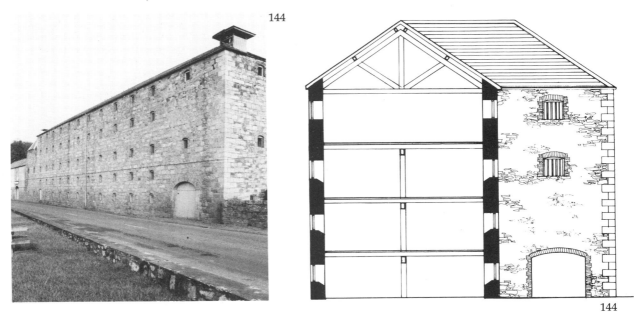

144

144 Muine Bheag, Co. Carlow – The Maltings, erected in 1868, still retains much of its original character; it was built in stone with timber floors and cast iron columns. The building is a good example of the nineteenth-century industrial buildings to be found in many towns, and indeed villages, throughout the country.

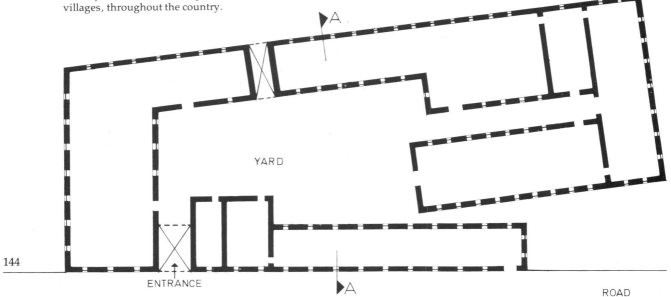

144

with any appreciation of their character. Industrial design has continued to evolve and today an industrial building is often indistinguishable from a school, a hospital or an office building.

A major social objective in both parts of Ireland is to transform the economy into a modern industrial one, avoiding over-reliance on agriculture and traditional industries. Industrial buildings are, therefore, an important new building type. Architectural styles are modern, and while the unevenness of standards common to modern development is still evident many new factories are architecturally interesting. Modern industrial buildings are now often considered as essentially a protection for extremely complex machinery, and so have become secondary to the processes involved, even more so than in the early days of the industrial revolution.

CANALS

Transportation, as it affects the architectural heritage of towns, concerns mainly the canals and railways. The canals, which were developed earlier than the railways, had a shorter life and were restricted in scale and location. Their major physical impact was more in the countryside than in the towns. Both systems have bequeathed a legacy of fine buildings, some of national significance, and almost all of local importance.

The first canal – Newry and Tyrone navigations – commenced in 1750. This waterway connected Newry, Co. Down, with Lough Neagh. The Grand Canal, which joins Dublin to the Shannon, was commenced in 1756. Later the Royal Canal, also connecting Dublin to the Shannon, but on a more northern alignment, was opened in 1789. Other canals were also built and existing waterways made more navigable, notably the Shannon, the Barrow and the Bann. The important buildings associated with the canal system were located in towns – harbours, warehouses, hotels and workers' housing. It was a time of fine building, excellent in design and craftsmanship. The standards achieved, while not attempting to reach the excellence and elegance of the large country and town houses, nevertheless convey a sense of Georgian proportions and simplicity. There was widespread use of dressed stone for many features, such as doorways, windows and quoins. The harbours were soundly built in stone, evidence

of which can still be seen today despite their neglect over the years. The hotels were pleasant buildings in the somewhat severe style of the smaller country house. They were designed as a basic convenience for overnight travellers, and were not considered suitable for long-term stays. The warehouses are superbly built in stone with the same general character, atmosphere and building techniques as contemporary mills and factories.

The canals had a relatively short active life because of the development of the railways, but for many years they continued on in a restricted manner. Indeed even after the commencement of the railways, canals were still being built. The Ulster Canal, linking the Erne and Blackwater, was opened in 1841. Many buildings still remain, often empty and unused, but all revealing that panache and style so typical of late eighteenth-century architecture.

RAILWAYS

The first railway was established in Ireland in 1834, running from Dublin to Kingstown, (later renamed Dun Laoghaire). There was a lull then for a few years, but in about 1845 the development of the railways began in earnest. By 1870 nearly two thousand miles of track had been laid. By any standards this was a marvellous achievement and it was of great social consequence, though the railways developed mainly on a commerical basis. The railway companies, now unified and nationalised, were initially separate commercial companies in competition with each other. However, they were in competition more for investments, rather than on actual routes, and like the banks they considered style and appearance important, if only to attract potential investors. Railway architecture assumed significance as in other European countries. For the architects, a railway commission was, like a bank, a prestigious job.

The main complex in a railway station, included a passenger hall, booking office, refreshment rooms, storage facilities, carriage sheds, workers' housing and perhaps an hotel. These were often developed in a single operation and at once added significantly to the architectural heritage of the town. The character of the railway station derived not only from the merit of the individual buildings, but from the pleasant overall atmosphere created by the relation-

145 Limerick city, Dock Road – Ranks Mill. Formerly Bannatyne's mill, Ranks is a sturdy and robust building typical of the period. It also exhibits interesting architectural details.

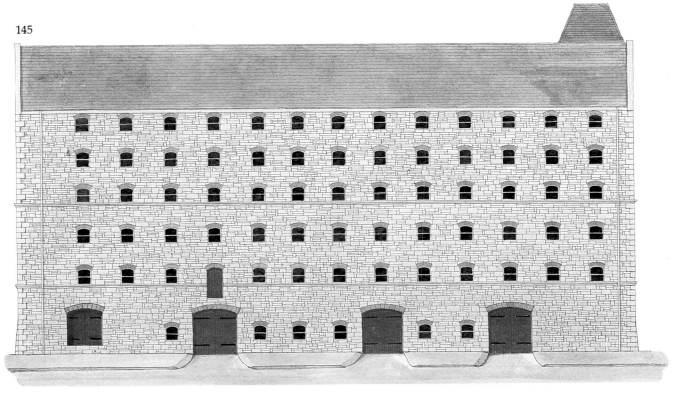

ELEVATION TO PLATFORM

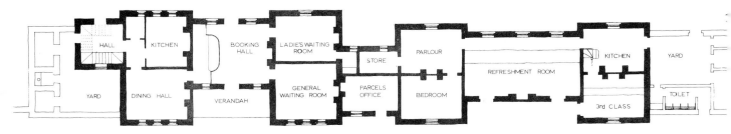

GROUND FLOOR PLAN

147

146 Clonmel, Co. Tipperary, Prior Park Road – railway station in classical style which also provides living accommodation. A high standard of workmanship is usually evident in such old railway buildings.

147 Ballymoney, Co. Antrim, Seymour Street – railway station. This building, erected towards the end of the nineteenth century, is in the arts and crafts style. It has changed very little in the intervening years and its essential features should now be preserved.

148 Moate, Co. Westmeath, Station Road – a small railway station in a classical style favoured at that time by the Great Western and Midland Railway Company. The great station on this line was the Broadstone in Dublin, (near King's Inns) architecturally one of the most distinctive of the great Dublin termini.

148

ship of the buildings to each other and the fine quality of materials used.

Dublin was the hub of the railway system, and the main terminus for most lines. This is reflected in the extremely high architectural quality of the Dublin stations. They were designed along classical lines, no doubt in response to the marvellous range of public buildings then existing in the city. The standard achieved in the country towns, although less grand, is of equal importance in its particular locality. The architectural styles of the provincial stations were varied, depending on the architect's choice or perhaps the view of the railway board – a not insignificant factor. A consistent design theme was often maintained throughout the company, although there was little standardisation of actual buildings. The classical and Gothic styles were most widely used. The Midland and Western railway company favoured a classical and the South Western a Gothic style, although it was never a hard and fast rule. For example, Clonmel, Co. Tipperary, although part of the South Western system, is in the classical style. Architecturally, railway stations are invariably interesting examples of the particular style. The use of high quality materials and superb standards of craftsmanship were commonplace. Brick and stone and in many cases cast iron were used to imaginative effect. Even the most ordinary boundary wall or bridge was built with a feeling for the material and a concern for craftsmanship. For years the local railway station was a hub of activity: all local comings and goings began there and the waiting rooms and booking halls were gay with coloured posters advertising the link between the small local station and a vast communications network which covered the world. Even the most exciting journey to far-away places would begin here; it was even possible to book through the local station. Fortunately the architecture of the railways measured up to the romanticism they evoked. Today a well-presented station complex – and only a few are still in operation – is a pleasant feature in any town.

The railway system is now a mere shadow of what it was. Only the main lines are still in operation, and even these are under threat. Many small stations have closed and some are now in private ownership and used for a variety of purposes, from dwelling houses to workshops. Occasionally the conversion has been carried through with sensitivity and appreciation of the individual architecture and of the unique atmosphere of the old station complex. In most cases, however, the quality of the original architecture is ignored.

Perhaps the present concern for the intelligent use of energy, which has increased the prospects for public transport, may mean a renaissance for the railways. It is no longer allowed to sell off a railway line, for instance, or even to take up the tracks. Today, 150 years or so after their first development, the basic concept of the railways remains valid. But even a renaissance is unlikely to mean a return to the superb quality of craftsmanship and use of fine materials which the railway companies achieved in the late nineteenth century. So it is all the more important to respect the buildings now existing. Sadly even the public railway companies are often unaware of this fine heritage. It is quite common for new railway buildings to be erected in shoddy materials with little feeling for their surroundings, and, which is perhaps more disappointing, for crude repairs to be carried out to superb examples of craftsmanship – a poor reflection on to-day's craftspeople, and an insult to their predecessors.

HARBOURS

In every era international trade was of importance, but particularly so from the eighteenth century onwards. Most international trading was carried out by sea until recent times. There are remnants of medieval harbours in Ireland, some of which were discovered during the Wood Quay excavations in Dublin, and there are probably more such discoveries yet to be made in other old ports.

In the nineteenth century there was a major programme of development and improvement of harbours because of increasing trade and also as part of public relief works. John Rennie, the engineer and harbour builder, designed the famous examples at Dun Laoghaire and at Donaghadee, Co. Down. A lesser known and now modernised harbour at Dunmore East in Co. Waterford is attributed to Alexander Nimmo. The harbours and their associated buildings were in the mainstream of industrial architecture of the period – simple, straightforward with few frills. They are marvellous examples of masonry work allied to brilliant engineering skills. The warehouses were robust and had a functional appearance, but other buildings,

149 Milford, Co. Donegal, Main Street – garage with a barrel-vaulted roof – often known as 'Belfast roof'. An unusual, stylised front, demonstrating that even the most ordinary of buildings can seek inspiration from the 'great architectural styles'.

150 Tipperary town, Railway Road – creamery. This early creamery is essentially a simple structure clad in iron. Nevertheless, it has a style influenced by the popular fashions of the time. It is an unusually attractive building.

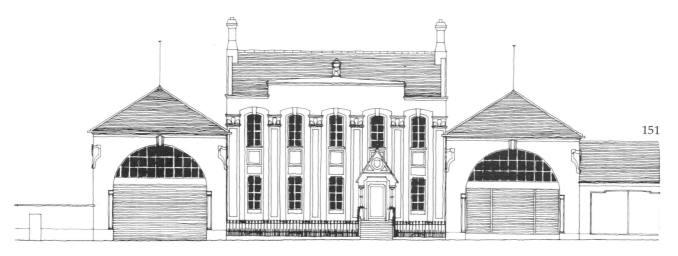

151 Dublin city, Lr. Rathmines Road – This former motor assembly plant is an early modern industrial building but influenced by traditional architectural styles which have given it a distinctive quality.

152 Dublin city, Lr. Rathmines Road – Kodak building. This factory and warehouse building, with its clearly expressed lines, is a good example of an early modern industrial building.
153 Dublin, Naas Road – a post-war factory, built for the Aspro company, which is modern in concept but retains a traditional image.

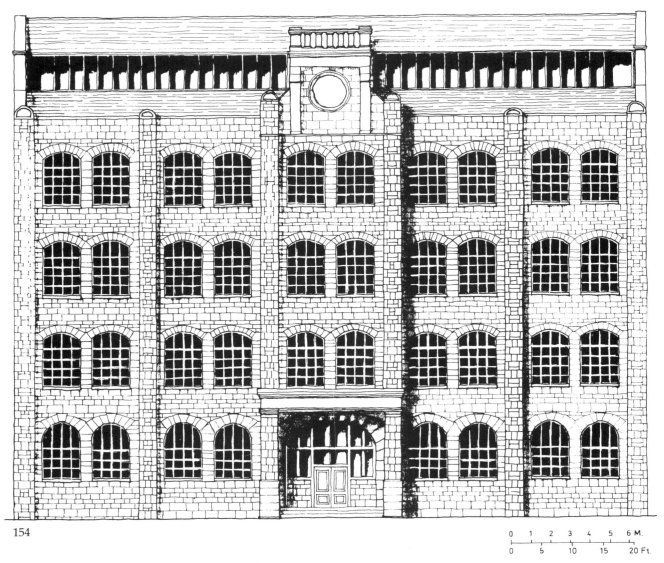

0 1 2 3 4 5 6 M.

0 5 10 15 20 Ft.

154 Derry city, Foyle Road – an impressive multi-storey factory – the extensive use of glass anticipates the modern styles, still to come.

such as the harbour master's office and the customs office always had a touch of elegance and style. The harbour walls were built with a sturdiness that makes a modern observer wonder how relatively simple building techniques could achieve such high standards. The lighthouses have a style and elegance which even the most sophisticated architecture today would find it hard to surpass.

Old harbours exude an atmosphere and charm which has a wide appeal despite their decaying appearance, disused warehouses, the weed-covered walls and pathways, the dead ship's hulk being slowly covered by the silting sand and perhaps here and there a notice indicating sailings to Glasgow, Liverpool or further afield. But they were not always like this. In years past they were

busy places with small ships importing coal, bricks and other materials, and exporting cattle, sheep, even people. It is hard to envisage the smaller ports ever being commercially viable again. Like other traditional transportation systems, shipping has become centralised. A few ports now control all the movements where formerly there were dozens. Dublin and Belfast are the giants. Some smaller ports have retained their identity through commercial fishing. Other ports have become industrial areas, with goods being transferred by land rather than by sea. The old buildings are usually hidden within a mix of modern sheds. Even so, their quality is still obvious, and many are worth restoring.

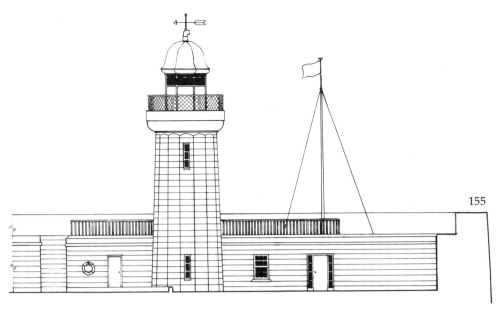

155

156

157

155 Dunmore East, Co. Waterford – This elegant lighthouse in the form of a Doric column is one of the few remaining structures of the original harbour attributed to Alexander Nimmo.

156 Leighlin, Co. Carlow – This graceful bridge over the river Barrow is typical of many such elegant structures built during the nineteenth century. They are now subject to severe pressure from heavy modern vehicles. Many have been insensitively widened in recent years.

157 Monasterevin, Co. Kildare – The canal harbour displays the tranquil atmosphere associated with old harbours. Assets like this should not be allowed to deteriorate particularly as we are on the threshold of a new 'leisure age'.

Chapter Eight

The Future

What does the future promise? Over the past two hundred years buildings of many types have been erected in our towns, buildings which cater for all kinds of activities, from day-to-day living which the dwelling house provides for, to the more formal occasions which take place in the churches, court-houses and other public buildings. The present phase of development commenced in the 1960s and is now in full swing. What architectural heritage will it leave?

It has been estimated that the total population on the entire island will be over five and a half million at the turn of the century – a mere seventeen years away. It is likely that between now and the end of the century as many new buildings will be erected as have been for the previous two hundred and fifty years. The great majority of the buildings will be ordinary ones, similar in range and purpose to what we have been discussing. Some building types will, undoubtedly, continue to be built. We will need family homes. It is difficult at this point in time to visualise an alternative social arrangement to the nuclear family or to the social aim that each household have a separate dwelling; our time span is too short to contemplate major changes. And we will need schools and recreational buildings to cater for a growing population.

Technology is also constantly changing, presenting new demands to architects. Modern hospitals and factories bear little resemblance to their older counterparts. The complex activities which take place in such buildings are considered to be of more importance than the buildings themselves. Coping with this problem is a great challenge to contemporary architecture.

There are other constraints at work nowadays which were absent in the past – society is more egalitarian and also more bureaucratic. We have a plethora of laws and regulations dealing with the planning of towns and the erection of buildings. Their objectives are diverse: some aim to conserve the existing heritage and make our towns and villages better places to live in; others are concerned with the actual requirements of buildings, and aesthetic or heritage matters are secondary.

It can be said that nearly every building is important in some way or other – to a family, as a record of their own past; to a small community, as a reminder of its history and of the social activities of former days. Buildings outlive their builders and often their original purpose; they are part of the continuity of every town. Architecture is a social art. The streets and buildings of any city or town, their condition, character and general appearance are important distinguishing marks of a community's attitude.

All buildings should aspire to architectural character. Few builders set out to purposely create ugly architecture although this may often be the result of their work. Ideally, a building should be suitable for its function, achieve a standard of craftsmanship appropriate to its use, have a rational architectural expression and respect the surroundings in which it is located.

How can we ensure that today's new buildings will in the main constitute a heritage of which future generations can be proud? It is hardly likely to come merely from the application of rules and regulations. It would not necessarily follow either that if all buildings were designed by architects then standards would rise dramatically. In the final analysis it will be a question of education in the broadest sense – not merely the training of more professionals and technicians but a general improvement in public awareness and in appreciation of our architectural heritage.

Whilst doing the surveys and field work carried out in preparation for this book we have been disappointed at people's general lack of knowledge of and appreciation for the buildings which they themselves may live or work in or which may be important in the social life of their community. However, despite this there are also encouraging signs of a new awareness of local heritage of which buildings are now seen as a part. A few years ago, ordinary buildings such as market houses and churches could be demolished arousing little public concern – a few individuals might perhaps mourn their passing. Today however, such a proposal will generate considerable debate at least. As many buildings become functionally obsolete, more effort is being made to find a more efficient use for them whilst simultaneously respecting the character of the building.

But there is a lot more to be done. Architecture has still to be widely accepted as an important aspect of local heritage comparable, for instance, to social and musical traditions. There is a wealth of knowledge to be gained from having a better understanding of the buildings in one's own town: they are part of its history and culture and may have more personal significance than more famous national buildings. In addition, where there is concern, knowledge, and appreciation of local architecture the great building will be less endangered. Learning about buildings and their craftsmanship, can be a rewarding experience – it is interesting, for example, to find out what influenced a particular design; what is the architectural style – was it part of a current fashion or was the building a trendsetter in its day; who were the original occupants and what was its purpose; who was responsible for construction; what materials were used and where did they come from; what craftsmen were involved – are there other examples of their work in the district? One might investigate the local forces at work in replacing the simple eighteenth-century churches with the impressive nineteenth-century Gothic revival buildings. This is the stuff local history is made of. Photographing, sketching and measuring buildings, as an individual

or as a group, could become an important cultural pursuit. Think of the contribution any local group would make towards a better understanding of their area if they measured and recorded the buildings in their own locality. This has been done but as yet only on a limited scale.

The Ulster Architectural Heritage Society founded in 1967 provides a particularly outstanding example of this kind of work. Despite all the social upheaval and physical disturbances, the Society has carried out and published surveys on many Ulster towns — all on a voluntary basis. These surveys deal with the whole nine counties of Ulster. They are comprehensive and include useful information about the architecture and history of particular buildings. They have been a valuable source of knowledge for local groups and have also been used widely by public authorities. In the South, there is not as yet the same dynamic approach to architectural records. An Foras Forbartha (The National Institute for Physical Planning) has compiled lists of architecturally significant buildings in certain counties. Some have been published and have contributed significantly to increasing public awareness in a particular locality. An Taisce (The National Trust for Ireland) has also published surveys with a strong emphasis on architectural matters. The most outstanding of these was a survey of Kilkenny city — perhaps among the most architecturally conscious towns in the country. The Historic Buildings Council in Northern Ireland records and lists various types of buildings, many of local significance. The Irish Architectural Archive in Dublin, founded in 1976, has established a collection of drawings, photographs and records of buildings, many of which are of local significance.

These activities, praiseworthy as they may be, are all in many ways selective. Architectural appreciation is not widely practised; perhaps it is too much to expect that it ever would be. However, a sense of taste and understanding about ordinary buildings, a feel for the manner in which they are constructed and how they relate to their surroundings could become a developed instinct in many people. It is not necessary to know all the architectural styles and theories or to be deeply knowledgeable about building technology. This is the field of the experts or the rare enthusiastic amateur. But most people are concerned about the appearance of their own home and often go to considerable expense to improve it, but unfortunately not always with the best of taste. This is due generally to a lack of knowledge rather than a lack of care. There is a great deal of work which schools and educational authorities could do. Local architecture, its significance and role, should have an important place in the school curriculum. It could be argued that an educational system which presents facts and figures about faraway places but ignores local traditions is somewhat blinkered. There is also much which could be done in extra-mural education to discover and assess aspects of local architecture.

It is likely that with changing occupations and the transition from agricultural to urban activities that the great majority of the future population will live in urban areas. The buildings which will cater for this increased urban population will be ordinary buildings similar to the types discussed in this book. The challenge before us is to increase the awareness of the ordinary individual about the significance and importance of local architecture – how it contributes to the quality of life and to the distinctive character of a town. We must engender a sense of pride in our surroundings. This is the stuff of which great civilisations are made and fine attitudes are handed on from one generation to another. The task is great, but we cannot shirk it.

A Simple Guide to Architectural Styles

Classical: The original influence was the architecture of the Greek and Roman civilisations. Having fallen out of favour during medieval times, it was revived from the thirteenth century onwards as part of the Italian Renaissance. In subsequent centuries the use of classical architecture spread throughout Europe. Its arrival in Ireland coincided with the physical development of the country in the seventeenth century, and it was widely used for all types of buildings in the eighteenth and nineteenth centuries, and with different variations up to the 1930s and 40s. It is the most dominant architectural style, at least for ordinary buildings. Its essential features are the use of classical elements: columns, pilasters, pediments, entablatures, cornices, square- or round-headed windows, architraves, shallow roofs, parapet walls, and restraint in the use of materials.

Gothic: Conceived originally in the Middle Ages, it was the predominant style for cathedrals, churches and public buildings. New development in structure allowed for larger window opes and lighter buildings. It went out of fashion during the great classical period of the seventeenth and eighteenth centuries, although towards the end of the eighteenth century Gothic influences began to re-emerge. It was fully revived as an important architectural style in the mid-nineteenth century, influenced by the writings and work of Augustus Welby Pugin, and was widely used for churches and public buildings. Indeed it was often considered the most appropriate style for ecclesiastical archi-

Classical (domestic)

Classical (public)

Gothic

tecture. Its essential features are the use of pointed windows and openings, often with elaborate tracery carried out in stone, intricate stone carving based on natural and religious features, steep roofs with towers and pinnacles.

Victorian: The Victorian period covers the latter part of the nineteenth century. There is no specific Victorian style as such: Victorian architecture incorporates elements from earlier styles. Perhaps it is best exemplified by a more vigorous approach to architecture, both in the form of buildings and the materials used, in contrast to the restraint of the classical period. This period also witnessed great improvements in transportation – principally railways. It was then easier to use building materials not actually produced locally; for example, brick and terracotta were widely used.

Domestic Tudor: As a consequence of the Gothic revival there was also a revival of interest in medieval domestic buildings. Although there were few if any timber-framed buildings then existing in Ireland, the Tudor style became quite popular for large and medium sized houses, and was widely used in the cities and larger towns, particularly at the turn of the century. It was then, of course, a widely used architectural style in Britain. The relevant features are leaded windows, plaster panels with timber framing, usually painted black and white, projecting windows and porches and high roofs.

Arts and Crafts: The arts and crafts movement was founded by William Morris and others towards the end of the nineteenth century. Essentially it was a reaction against the overstandardisation of machine-made products from the industrial revolution. It sought its inspiration in the high quality and craft work of earlier periods. The movement influenced architecture, particularly in the domestic field. It looked backwards to earlier forms, particularly the English cottage and used high roofs, small windows, nooks and projecting porches and conveyed a romantic picturesque feeling. The use of gable fronts also became popular which allowed opportunities for intricate design forms, in many cases inspired by Dutch architectural styles of the sixteenth and seventeenth centuries.

Art Nouveau: Generally a development of the arts and crafts style, distinguished by the use of intricate decorative features based on natural motifs – flowers, animals, etc.

Italianate: Associated mainly with domestic buildings and only to a lesser extent used in public buildings. Its major influence were the large town houses or palaces erected by Italian Renaissance princes, which were in turn inspired by classical ideas. Essential features are a dis

Victorian

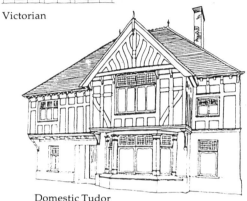

Domestic Tudor

Arts and Crafts

Art Nouveau

tinctive use of plaster for mouldings, cornices and other details, windows and openings in the classical style, more formal in expression than the Tudor or arts and crafts styles. Popular from the mid-nineteenth century onwards and often a feature of seaside towns where the use of highly coloured plaster facades was quite common.

Modern: The modern style began with the industrial buildings of the nineteenth century. Then, often perhaps from necessity, ornamentation and any architectural extravagances were omitted. The nature of the building was strongly influenced by the technology necessary in the industrial process. The development of the modern style was also helped by the new building techniques of structural steel and reinforced concrete, which allowed more flexibility in the planning of buildings. Early modern architects, such as Le Corbusier, considered that architecture has a role in breaking down and equalising existing class differences.

Though it was a style occasionally used in the 1920s and 1930s, it was not until after the war that the modern style became the predominant architectural fashion. The essential feature of the modern style is the absence of ornamentation of any sort, the use of large expanses of glass and flat roofs, particularly for public buildings. The pitched roof has still remained predominantly popular in domestic architecture. Since the war the modern style has been almost universally used for all the modern office blocks and other public buildings erected in the cities and larger towns.

Pastiche: The name associated with a widespread trend in recent years in both commercial and domestic building of copying past styles, principally the classical town houses of the eighteenth century. The style has evolved because of a general public reaction against modern architecture particularly its impact on existing cities and towns.

However, to be carried out successfully, pastiche requires a deep knowledge and appreciation of the particular architectural style used. Dressing up a twentieth-century office to look like an eighteenth century townhouse is, in most situations, a contradiction.

Post Modern: This is the name given to the most recent development in architecture, which, though eschewing a wholly pastiche approach to buildings, seeks to use details and methods from classical or Gothic styles in an individual way, but still reflecting the modern function of buildings. Such use of ornamentation and details from past styles is fashionable.

Italianate

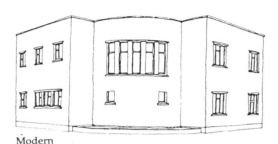

Modern

Pastiche

Post Modern

158

158 Dublin city, Dame Court – The Stag's
Head. The Stag's Head is a fine example of
Victorian pub architecture. Built in 1899 on
the site of a former pub, the facade is of
finely carved stone, polished granite and
brickwork. The interior is a stunningly
exciting essay of the period – superb
mahogany fittings, high-quality stained
glass. It is a tribute to remarkable craftwork
and an indication of the design qualities which pub owners were prepared to
aspire to.

The Illustrations: date, architect and builder (where known)

Many buildings illustrated may not have been formally designed in the generally accepted sense, therefore it was not always possible to obtain specific information about them.
Where possible we note the architect, the builder or persons associated with the original building who might be expected to have influenced its design.

In each case we list the illustration number, date, the architect (a.), the builder (b.).

1, 1890, W. J. Watson a.
2, 1847, Sancton Wood a.
4, demolished 1812
5, 1880s
7, 1310
12, 1603
15, Court-house, W. V. Morrison a.
17, 1880 J. L. Robinson a., Michael Meade & Son b.
22, 1780
24, 1792, Jackson family b.
26, 1820, Farnham Estate b.
27, 1568, Nicholas Shee b.
28, *circa* 1450
29, 1842, William Reed a., (perhaps from standard plan), William Reed b.
34, 1570, demolished 1824, Nicholas Bathe b.
38, 1879, Lord Blayney, b.
40, 1896, Stringer b.
41, 1795-1805, Robert Day b.
44, 1840, church
50, 1853, J. Tinkler b.
53, 1902
54, 1912, Kenny b.
55, 1934, Rupert Jones a., John Kenny b.
59, 1938
61, 1834
62, 1817
64, 1912
66, 1812, James Sheane a.
67, 1845, Sir John Young b.
68, 1942, E. P. O'Flynn a., Coveneys Cork b.
69, C. R. Cockerell
70, 1900, Messrs. Carroll of Bachelor a.
71, 1838 – 42, G. Wilkinson
72, 1838 – 42, G. Wilkinson
73, 1756, Col. Hugh Boyd b.
74, 1853
76, 1833, William Murray
77, 1821, Portico 1845
79, 1839, Millar a.
80, 1862, Sir John Benson a., Thomas Walsh b.
81, 1906, Iveagh Trust b.
82, 1893, A. Scott a., T. Reilly b.
83, 1832, Rev. Samuel Ian Montgomery b.
84, 1879, Thomas Cleary, foreman (local labour)
85, *circa* 1790, Francis Johnston a.
86, 1932, Mr Brady O.P.W. a.

87, 1840s
90, 1843, John B. Keane a., John Hanly b.
92, 1866, Wm. Hague a., Crowe Bros. b.
93, 1910, W. A. Scott a., W. M. Callaghan b.
94, 1905, Patrick & Francis Duffy
95, 1850, reconstructed 1904, John Lacret b.
96, 1905, George L. O'Connor a., Michael Heeney b.
97, 1927
98, 1904
101, 1892, J. K. Freeman a., Michael Lynch b. for Rev. William Fortune C.C.
102, 1900, D. Sheridan a.
104, 1903, P. J. Lynch O.P.W. a., P. Costen b.
105, 1909, J. Crowe O.P.W. a.
106, Partly 1728, tower 1809
109, 1888-92, Lt. Col. J. T. Marsh a.
112, 1831
113, 1839-42, J. B. Keane a., John Hanly b.
116, 1936, Michael Scott & Good a., Collon Bros b.
118, Rebuilt 1890s, Robert McArdell a.
119, 1775, rebuilt 1875, Morrisey family a.
120, 1926, Shaw family a., C. Doyle b.
124, 1929
125, 1928
126, 1931, J. Medcalfe a., O'Connor & Bailey b.
127, 1875
128, 1868, S. Symes
129, 1860, S. Symes
131, 1923
136, 1919, McDonnell & Dixon a., John Hearne & Sons b.
140, 1912
143, 1839 onwards to 1940, John Locke with Fallon and Brett b.
145, 1873, J. M. Bannatyne b.
147, 1901, Berkelay D. Wise a., iron work McFarlane's Glasgow
148, 1845
149, 1925, John McMahon a., John McMahon b.
152, 1932
153, Alan Hope a., G. & T. Crampton b.
154, 1899
155, 1825, Alexander Nimno
157, 1790, Grand Canal Company b.
159, 1826, demolished 1937, John Killaly a., Mullen, McMahon & Henry b.

Bibliography

Breffny, Brian de, and Ffolliott, Rosemary, *Houses of Ireland*, London, 1975.

Brett, C.E.B., *Buildings of Belfast 1700-1914*, London, 1967.

Brett, C.E.B., *Court Houses and Market Houses of the Province of Ulster*, Belfast.

Ulster Architectural Heritage Society (UAHS), 1973.

Butlin R. A. Ed., *The Development of the Irish Town*, London, 1977.

Camblin, G., *The Town in Ulster*, Belfast, 1951.

Craig, Maurice, *Dublin 1660-1860*, 1952. Reprinted Dublin 1969 and 1980.

Craig, Maurice, *Classic Irish Houses of the Middle Size*, London, 1976.

Craig, Maurice, *History of Irish Architecture*, London, 1982.

Cullen, L. M.. *Life in Ireland*, London, 1968.

Cullen, L. M., *Irish Towns and Villages*, Dublin, 1979.

Danaher, Kevin, *Irish Vernacular Architecture*, Cultural Relations Committee, Dublin, 1975.

Delaney, V. T. & D. R. *The Canals of the South of Ireland*, Newton Abbot, 1966.

Dixon, Hugh, *An Introduction to Ulster Architecture*, UAHS, Belfast, 1975.

Foras Forbartha, An (National Institute of Physical Planning and Research), architectural surveys of most counties and certain towns not published but sometimes available in local libraries or from the institute. The surveys form part of the National Heritage Inventory. Published surveys cover Cobh, Kinsale, Carlow, Tullamore, Bray and Ennis.

Evans, David, *An Introduction to Modern Architecture in Ulster*, Belfast, UAHS, 1977.

Evans, David and Patton, Marcus, *The Diamond as big as a Square _ An Introduction to Towns and Buildings in Ulster*, UAHS, Belfast, 1981.

Freeman, T. W., *Pre-Famine Ireland*, Manchester, 1957.

Georgian Society, *Records of Eighteenth-Century Domestic Architecture in Dublin*, Dublin, 1909. Reprinted 1969.

Green, E.R.R., *Industrial Archaeology of Co. Down*, HMSO, London, 1963.

Harbison, Peter, Potterton, Homan, and Sheehy, Jeanne, *Irish Art and Architecture*, London, 1978.

Lanigan, Katherine and Tyler, Gerald, *Kilkenny – Its Architecture and History*, An Taisce, Dublin, 1977.

Leask, H. J., *Irish Churches and Monastic Buildings Vols. 1,2,3*. Dundalk, 1955.

Lewis, Samuel, *A topographical Dictionary of Ireland*, 2 vols and atlas, 1837.

Maxwell, C. E., *Town and Country in Ireland under the Georges*, London, 1940 and *Dublin under the Georges*, London, 1936.

McCutcheon, W. A., *The Industrial Archaeology of Northern Ireland*, HMSO, Belfast, 1981.

MacDermott, M. J., *Ireland's Architectural Heritage*, Dublin, 1975.

McLysaght, E., *Irish Life in the Seventeenth Century*, 1939. Republished Dublin 1979.

MacNamara, T. F., *Portrait of Cork*, Cork, 1981.

McParland, Edward, 'The Wide Streets Commissioners' in *Irish Georgian Society Bulletin*, Jan.-March, Dublin, 1972.

O'Dwyer, Frederick, *Lost Dublin*, Dublin, 1981.

Potterton, Homan, *Irish Church Monuments*, London, 1975.

Rothery, Sean, *The Shops of Ireland*, Dublin, 1978.

Rothery, Sean, *Everyday Buildings of Ireland*, Dublin, 1975.

Rowan, Alistair, *The Buildings of Ireland, North West Ulster*, London, 1979. The first in a projected series to cover the entire island (contains a comprehensive glossary of architectural terms).

Shaffrey, Patrick, *The Irish Town*, Dublin, 1975.

Sheehy, Jeanne, *J. J. McCarthy and the Gothic Revival in Ireland*, UAHS Belfast, 1977.

Sheehy, Jeanne, *The Rediscovery of Ireland's Past – The Celtic Revival 1830-1930*, London, 1980.

Ulster Architectural Heritage Society architectural surveys of most Ulster towns, from 1967 onwards.

Wilkinson, George, *Practical Geology and Ancient Architecture of Ireland*, London and Dublin, 1845 (architecture of the workhouses).

159 Tullamore, Co. Offaly, Cormac Street – jail. An impressive and intimidating entrance, now the entrance to a factory.

ENTRANCE

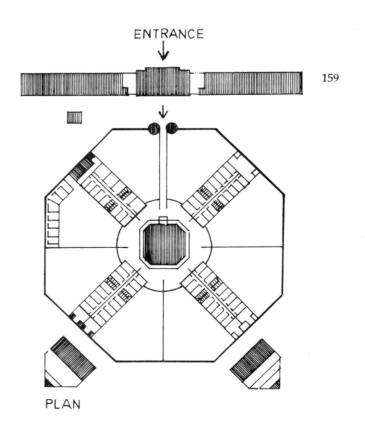

159

PLAN

DATE DUE

GAYLORD PRINTED IN U.S.A